THINKING CONNECTIONS

Learning to Think and Thinking To Learn

This program was developed through a collaboration between the Project Zero Cognitive Skills Group of Harvard University and the Northeast Regional Educational Laboratory.

Authors

David N. Perkins, Heidi Goodrich, and Shari Tishman of Harvard University, and Jill Mirman Owen of the Northeast Regional Educational Laboratory

Addison-Wesley Publishing Company

Menlo Park, California • Reading, Massachusetts • New York
Don Mills, Ontario • Wokingham, England • Amsterdam
Bonn • Sydney • Singapore • Tokyo • Madrid • San Juan
Paris • Seoul, Korea • Milan • Mexico City • Taipei, Taiwan

Editorial Director: *Patricia Brill*
Editor: *Carol Callahan*
Production Editor: *Sandra Sella Raas*
Production/Manufacturing Director: *Janet Yearian*
Production/Manufacturing Coordinator: *Leanne Collins*
Design Manager: *Jeff Kelly*
Text and Cover Design: *Christy Butterfield*
Poster Design: *Terry Guyer*

Acknowledgments

The authors would like to thank Michael Farady, who was extensively involved in the development of an earlier version of this material; Kate Wilson for her design assistance; Susan Loucks-Horsely for her thoughtful feedback; the John T. and Catherine D. MacArthur Foundation and the Spencer Foundation for their support of the work of David Perkins and his colleagues at Harvard Graduate School of Education.

The authors would also like to express their gratitude to students, teachers, and administrators in Arlington, Massachusetts; Burrilville, Rhode Island; Cambridge, Massachusetts; Fairfield, Vermont; and Winchester, Massachusetts for their help in pilot testing this program.

Cover Credits

Top Left: NASA Johnson Space Center
Top Right: Culver Pictures
Top Middle: Stephen Frisch
Bottom Middle: Stephen Frisch
Bottom Left: Joe Viesti/Viesti Associates, Inc.

ISBN 0-201-81998-8
12 11 10 9 8 7 6 5 4 -M L- 03 02 01 00

CONTENTS

INTRODUCTION

Welcome to Thinking Connections

Reading, Writing, Mathematics, Social Studies, Science, Health, Physical Education, Art—all of these subjects have important places in the school curriculum. As a teacher, you want students to gain knowledge in each area of study. You also want them to develop thinking skills and study habits that will last a lifetime.

It is no surprise to teachers that students don't always think as well as they might. Students often have trouble thinking through such things as solving a word problem in mathematics, or understanding the main idea in a paragraph, or deciding whether good health habits and activities are important to them. This program will guide you in helping students learn to think—and think to learn.

Thinking Connections is a thinking strategies program that teaches critical and creative thinking within the context of your regular curriculum. It will help students *learn to think* by teaching them specific skills and strategies. At the same time, it will help students *think to learn* by teaching them how to systematically work through various learning tasks and topics. Acquiring such skills will help students in the classroom and in their everyday, out-of-the-classroom lives.

Why Thinking Connections?

This program is based on certain underlying beliefs. If you share some or all of these beliefs, we think that you will find *Thinking Connections* to be an interesting and useful tool of instruction.

We believe that all students can learn to be better thinkers and learners and that they can develop positive attitudes toward thinking and learning. Even though it is widely known that ALL students need to develop better skills in order to be successful in the world of tomorrow, thinking skills programs tend to be targeted for gifted students in many schools today. All students—including those at risk of failure, low achievers, and those with learning disabilities—can learn higher order skills. Research supports this conclusion. Everyone can learn how to brainstorm creative ideas, seek evidence to support their beliefs, consider the viewpoints of others, and so on.

We believe that thinking things through is always important in learning any subject matter. When students have a chance to think critically and creatively about what they are learning, knowledge becomes more meaningful to them. Their retention is greater and they are better able to relate what they learn to other topics and activities in and out of school.

Research shows that the thoughtful working through, or elaborative processing, of the sort introduced in decision making, understanding, and other thinking skill strategies can result in deeper learning. Students learn through experience that thinking and learning are engaging and rewarding pursuits.

We believe that teaching thinking is an excellent way to integrate different subject matter. Since thinking should be part of every subject, the teaching of thinking strategies provides an excellent way to connect subject matter to one another. There exist natural connections between different areas of the curriculum. Thinking strategies that are not subject bound enable teachers to make connections among the various topics and concepts that they teach both within and across disciplines and experiences.

Does Thinking Connections *Work?*

This program has been used by teachers at all grade levels and formally tested at grades three through six. The material has undergone revisions based on classroom observation and on the suggestions made by teachers who used the program with their students during regular classroom instruction. On the basis of this research and experience, we can say that:

- *Thinking Connections* is very teachable. After familiarizing themselves with the material and teaching the initial lessons, teachers find that the practices are engaging to teach and move along quite smoothly.

- Students respond well to *Thinking Connections*. Even very young students are generally responsive to the practices and absorb the strategies readily.

- Students sharpen their thinking skills. After the initial twelve weeks of using this program (teaching all three strategies) and reinforcing the concepts and strategies on a regular basis thereafter, students DO improve their thinking and score higher on thinking skills tests.

- Teachers improve their own thinking skills as well as their teaching. Teachers have mentioned that they become increasingly aware of their own thinking processes as they work through this program with their students. Once teachers internalize the steps in the strategies, they know that they, as well as their students, have the power to apply the strategies across the curriculum and in their daily lives.

The Thinking Strategies

There are three modules in this program. Each module teaches one thinking strategy. A short overview of each module is presented below.

Module One: The Mental Management Strategy

This strategy helps students develop an increased awareness of their own thinking process and their control over it as they engage in a pre-task mental planning step and two post-task steps involving transfer of knowledge and reflection. Students will also have a better understanding of the actual task, the material with which they are using the strategy.

Pre-Task Step: Get Ready In this step, students take a few seconds to focus their thoughts, remember the last time that they did a similar task, and form mental images of the task or topic they will be addressing. The purpose of this step is to get students into a prepared and focused state of mind prior to beginning the task.

First Post-Task Step: Make Connections Immediately after completing the task, students make connections to other areas of knowledge and to their own experiences. The purpose of this step is to explicitly foster the transfer of both content knowledge and thinking skills.

Second Post-Task Step: Think About Thinking During this step, students review and assess the task just completed by identifying which parts of the experience went well and which parts were difficult. Then students consider how they can improve their performance in the future. The purpose of this step is to make students aware of their own thought processes and of the fact that they have the power to improve them.

Module Two: The Decision-Making Strategy

Module Two introduces students to the Decision-Making Strategy. Decision making is an important part of everyone's life—now and in the future. Students not only think through their own decisions but also decisions made by real people and imaginary characters. Students explore and come to a better understanding of important topics in the curriculum by using the decision-making strategy to think through historical, literary, and current decision points. The strategy is composed of the three powerful questions briefly presented below.

First Question: What Are the Options? Too often people choose from an unnecessarily limited set of solutions at decision points because they don't think beyond the obvious "either-or" options. The purpose of this step is to teach students to look beyond the obvious options by generating numerous and creative alternatives.

Second Question: What Are the Reasons? After generating a list of options, students select the most promising ones and give complete reasons, both pro and con, for each one. The two main purposes of this step are to combat faulty thinking habits (thinking only of reasons on the pro side for a favorite option, for example) and to teach students to carefully evaluate many options before making a final decision.

Third Question: What Is the Best Choice? During this step, students again consider the most promising options and decide which option is best supported by important reasons—and why. The purpose of this step is to teach students to make realistic and thoughtful decisions that are backed by complete and important reasons.

Module Three: Understanding Through Design

This strategy provides a systematic approach to learning for deep understanding. It does so by treating things, concepts, and events as "designs." Students explore the relationships between the purposes for each design and its features or parts. To do this probing, students again use three powerful questions that are briefly explained below. This strategy teaches students to analyze almost anything in a profound and systematic way so that they can better understand it.

First Question: What Are the Purposes? Students learn to look at and think deeply about the purposes of things, both tangible and intangible. This step encourages students to stretch their thinking beyond obvious or key purposes of a design to varied, creative, or hidden ones.

Second Question: What are the Features and Reasons? During this step, students consider the parts, materials, or characteristic features of a design and consider the reasons why the design has these features, or how the features help serve the purposes of the design. Completing this step will help students understand the connection between the features of something and how these features contribute to the purposes of that particular design.

Third Question: How Well Does It Work? After students understand how the features are connected to the purpose of a design, they are in a position to question the effectiveness of the design itself. The purpose of this step is to teach students to think critically as well as creatively in order to understand something, evaluate it, and make suggestions for possible improvements.

Teaching with Thinking Connections

Across the Curriculum

Thinking Connections fits comfortably into any area of the curriculum because of its built-in infusion approach. As you plan lessons for the various subjects, you can choose topics within subject matter where a strategy, or part of it, can enhance learning. We know a great deal about the teaching of thinking, but you are the expert on the important areas in your curriculum, your students' needs, and your personal teaching style. You can choose to infuse the strategies where they will work best for you and your students.

For your initial experience with this program, we strongly suggest that you follow the daily practices that are outlined later in this manual. Afterwards, you will be able to select where you want to infuse a strategy or selected steps from one or two strategies. The entries in the Sample Planner below illustrate some of the diverse ways in which all or part of the strategies can be infused into a daily curriculum after you and your students have mastered the basic elements of this program.

Sample Planner

MONDAY

SUBJECT/TOPIC: Social Studies—the Aztecs

STRATEGY: Decision-Making

Decision Point: Whether or not archaeological artifacts should be allowed to be taken from their country of origin

■ What are the options? (as many as possible)

■ What are the complete reasons? (pros and cons)

TUESDAY

SUBJECT/TASK: Spelling—taking a spelling quiz

STRATEGY: Mental Management

■ Pre-task: prepare to take the quiz (pause, remember, imagine)

■ Post-task: reflect on taking the quiz (what went well, what was hard, and what could be done better next time)

WEDNESDAY

SUBJECT/TOPIC: Science—fresh water ponds

STRATEGY: Understanding Through Design

The Design: the ecosystem of a pond

■ What purposes does it serve? (include non-obvious ones)

■ What are its features or parts? (and the reasons for them)

■ How well does it work? (how could it work better)

THURSDAY

SUBJECT/TASK: Language Arts—reading "Jack and the Beanstalk"

STRATEGY: Mental Management

■ Get Ready before reading the story

STRATEGY: Decision-Making

Decision Point: Should Jack have traded the the cow for the beans?

■ What were his options?

■ What decision would you have made in Jack's place? Why?

FRIDAY

SUBJECT/TOPIC: Art—Impressionism

STRATEGY: Understanding Through Design

The Design: Monet's painting,"Water Lilies" (an example of Impressionism)

■ What are the purposes and features of this painting?

■ How well does the painting work? Why?

Getting Started

Take some time to review the Table of Contents, read through this Introduction, and flip through the sections of this manual. As you look through the modules, you will notice that each contains the following mini-lessons that have been designed to be infused into your daily curriculum.

An Orientation Lesson This initial lesson introduces you and your students to the strategy and provides an overview of how the strategy works.

Concentrated Practices These shorter lessons focus on the specific steps of the strategy and allow students to work with each individual step on actual tasks or topics that they are studying.

Pulling It All Together Practices These lessons integrate all of the steps of the strategy and provide students with many opportunities to use the entire strategy on a task or topic from the curriculum.

The lessons and practices in this program have been designed to provide structure as well as flexibility. Each lesson plan supplies:

■ an overview page with step-by-step directions for preparing to teach the lesson

■ a Classroom Guide that offers step-by-step directions for conducting the lesson or practice, followed by an example of how that lesson might develop in your classroom

■ an After-the-Lesson Checklist to briefly review the effectiveness of each lesson or practice

■ some questions from teachers (like you) and answers from us that represent actual exchanges that have occurred during the development and testing of each step of this program.

Always remember to read through the materials completely before conducting your lessons. The lesson plans in this program offer examples, options, and suggestions for questions, discussions, teacher modeling, and so on. Only you can decide what will work best for you and your students, so take the time to prepare. As you work through the materials, you will become more familiar with the process and your lessons will require less preparation.

When you are ready to begin, simply turn to page 1 of the Mental Management module and follow the directions! One last word before you begin: It is always a challenge to start something new. Naturally, you want to be familiar with the materials. Don't expect yourself to be an expert before— or even after—teaching the first lesson. Rather, we recommend that you relax and enjoy learning the strategies along with your students.

The Time Frame

Each of the modules is designed to be taught over a period of four weeks. During the first week of each module, you will be presenting the Orientation Lesson for the strategy and conducting short practice sessions on the remaining days for the first step of the strategy.

During the second week, you and your students will be practicing a specific skill or skills in the second step of the strategy for a short time each day. The third week will be similarly spent with the third step. In the final and fourth week, you will guide students through the complete strategy, using all steps to gain experience in using the entire process.

The following calendar provides an overview of the time frame for teaching the entire twelve weeks (all three strategies) in this program. After this initial twelve weeks, it is up to you to pick and choose key places in the curriculum to introduce a step or a strategy, or to occasionally remind students to use their thinking skills when discussing a topic or approaching a task.

THINKING CONNECTIONS

A TWELVE-WEEK CALENDAR

		STRATEGY	MONDAY	TUESDAY	WEDNESDAY	THURSDAY	FRIDAY
MODULE ONE	WEEK 1	Mental Management	Orientation Lesson *40 minutes*	Get Ready Practice *10 minutes*	Get Ready Practice *4 minutes*	Get Ready Practice *4 minutes*	Get Ready Practice *4 minutes*
	WEEK 2	Mental Management	Make Connections Practice *20 minutes*	Make Connections Practice *15 minutes*	Make Connections Practice *15 minutes*	Make Connections Practice *15 minutes*	Make Connections Practice *15 minutes*
	WEEK 3	Mental Management	Think About Thinking Practice *20 minutes*	Think About Thinking Practice *15 minutes*	Think About Thinking Practice *15 minutes*	Think About Thinking Practice *15 minutes*	Think About Thinking Practice *15 minutes*
	WEEK 4	Mental Management	Pulling It All Together Practice *20 minutes*	Pulling It All Together Practice *20 minutes*	Pulling It All Together Practice *20 minutes*	Pulling It All Together Practice *20 minutes*	Pulling It All Together Practice *20 minutes*
MODULE TWO	WEEK 5	Decision-Making	Orientation Lesson *40 minutes*	What Are the Options? Practice *20 minutes*	What Are the Options? Practice *20 minutes*	What Are the Options? Practice *20 minutes*	What Are the Options? Practice *20 minutes*
	WEEK 6	Decision-Making	What Are the Reasons? Practice *40 minutes*	What Are the Reasons? Practice *20 minutes*	What Are the Reasons? Practice *20 minutes*	What Are the Reasons? Practice *20 minutes*	What Are the Reasons? Practice *20 minutes*
	WEEK 7	Decision-Making	What Is the Best Choice? Practice *20 minutes*	*(no practice)*	What Is the Best Choice? Practice *20 minutes*	*(no practice)*	What Is the Best Choice? Practice *20 minutes*
	WEEK 8	Decision-Making	Pulling It All Together Practice *45 minutes*	*(no practice)*	Pulling It All Together Practice *45 minutes*	*(no practice)*	Pulling It All Together Practice *45 minutes*

		STRATEGY	MONDAY	TUESDAY	WEDNESDAY	THURSDAY	FRIDAY
MODULE THREE	WEEK 9	Understanding Through Design	Orientation Lesson *40 minutes*	What Are the Purposes? Practice *15 minutes*	What Are the Purposes? Practice *15 minutes*	What Are the Purposes? Practice *15 minutes*	What Are the Purposes? Practice *15 minutes*
	WEEK 10	Understanding Through Design	What Are the Features and Reasons? Practice *20 minutes*	What Are the Features and Reasons? Practice *20 minutes*	What Are the Features and Reasons? Practice *20 minutes*	What Are the Features and Reasons? Practice *20 minutes*	What Are the Features and Reasons? Practice *20 minutes*
	WEEK 11	Understanding Through Design	How Well Does It Work? Practice *40 minutes*	*(no practice)*	How Well Does It Work? Practice *40 minutes*	*(no practice)*	How Well Does It Work? Practice *40 minutes*
	WEEK 12	Understanding Through Design	Pulling It All Together Practice *40 minutes*	*(no practice)*	Pulling It All Together Practice *40 minutes*	*(no practice)*	Pulling It All Together Practice *40 minutes*

1 | *The Mental Management Strategy*

Module One: *Overview*

Module One teaches a dynamic strategy for managing the thinking process. The strategy involves working through three basic steps or parts of the process. These steps are:

1. Get Ready
2. Make Connections
3. Think About Thinking.

Get Ready is a pre-task step. In this step students prepare their minds for a task, such as writing an essay, taking a quiz, or working on a project. After students have completed the task, they learn two post-task steps. In the second step students use what they already know to Make Connections with the present task. And in the final step, Think About Thinking, students reflect upon the high and low points of their thinking performances. They try to determine ways to improve upon their thinking the next time that they perform a similar task.

The Mental Management Strategy can be used as a strategy of its own or it can be infused into the daily classroom curriculum and other activities. It can also be used in combination with the Decision-Making and Understanding Through Design Strategies which are presented in Modules Two and Three.

In order that both teachers and students become familiar with the Mental Management Strategy, it is suggested that some time each day be used to present and practice the strategy for a period of four weeks as outlined below.

Suggested Timetable for Module One

WEEK 1 Monday: **Orientation Lesson** *(40 minutes)*
Tuesday: **Get Ready Practice** *(10 minutes)*
Wednesday – Friday: **Practice** *(2 minutes twice each day)*

WEEK 2 Monday: **Make Connections Practice** *(20 minutes)*
Tuesday – Friday: **Practice** *(15 minutes each day)*

WEEK 3 Monday: **Think About Thinking Practice** *(20 minutes)*
Tuesday – Friday: **Practice** *(15 minutes each day)*

WEEK 4 Monday – Friday: **Pulling It All Together Practice**
(20 minutes each day)

ORIENTATION LESSON

Purpose of this Lesson

The Orientation Lesson allows students to experience how the Mental Management Strategy can help them prepare for, work on, and reflect on a specific task. Since this lesson is intended to give students an overview of how the entire process works, students may not be able to complete the task assigned in this lesson. You may wish to give them time to do so later.

Preparation

■ Two sample Orientation Lessons are provided as models for your use. Each presents a different task to be done by the students: writing a story and memorizing the Preamble to the Constitution. Both lessons provide an overview of how the strategy might develop in your classroom. Decide which task to use with your students. Then read through the Writing Lesson that begins on the next page or the Memorizing Lesson that begins on page 7.

■ The Classroom Guide on page 12 provides an abbreviated lesson plan which you may find useful in reviewing your lesson strategy and conducting this lesson.

■ If you choose to use the Memorizing Lesson, make copies of the Preamble to the Constitution (see page 35) to give to your students.

■ Display the Mental Management poster in a prominent place in the classroom.

■ All suggested lesson plans in this manual assume that chalkboard and chalk or chart paper and a marker are available to record student responses.

Approximate Classroom Time Needed

WEEK 1   Monday: *40 minutes* divided as follows:

5 minutes for **Get Ready**, the pre-task step

20 minutes for the actual task

15 minutes for **Make Connections** and

Think about Thinking, the post-task steps

The Writing Lesson

1. Direct attention to the poster.

Read the title of the poster: The Mental Management Strategy. Ask a volunteer to tell what the word *strategy* means. (Possible answer: *A plan or method or series of steps used to reach a particular goal or result.*) If necessary, offer the clue that a strategy is a necessary step in sports such as football and in military operations. Have students read the poster copy.

Point out that the things listed on the poster tell about certain actions that anyone can take to make thinking more meaningful and memorable. The actions in thinking are a lot like playing a sport because you get better at it if you plan what to do, then practice doing it.

Ask, "When might you do a better job of thinking?" (Possible answers: *In reading, so I understand as I go along; in studying, so that I remember later on; in writing stories, so I get better ideas before I write; in thinking about how something I learned in class can be useful some other time;* and so on.)

Tell students that what they just named are all thinking situations. Explain that the Mental Management Strategy will help them by providing a method or plan to use before they do something in order to proceed wisely and avoid problems. It will also help them to analyze success or failure after the task is done in order to improve their performance.

Ask, "Why do you think the authors selected a sandwich as a comparison for this strategy?" (Possible answer: *One slice of bread is like the first step in planning, the filling is like the thinking task, and the other slice of bread is like what you do after the thinking task. They all go together.*)

2. Explain the Get Ready step.

Tell students that they will be using the Mental Management Strategy to help them write a story entitled "Moving to the Moon." They will begin by doing a pre-task step called *Get Ready.*

Say something like, "You can see from the poster that the first step you should take before you begin the task is to get ready for it. The Get Ready step has three parts: pause, remember, and imagine. *Pause* means to stop briefly. During that time, you clear your minds in order to concentrate on the task you are about to begin. You can close your eyes or put your head on your desk if it will help you concentrate."

Explain that *remember* means to think back to the last time you did a similar task, in this case wrote a story, and think about how you can do it even better this time. Ask questions like the following to help students do this.

Ask, "What did you do the last time you wrote a story that was really good or helpful?" Accept and record students' answers on the board or chart. Suggest that they remember to repeat these actions today.

Then ask, "What did you do the last time that didn't work or that made the task harder?" Again, accept and record answers. Remind students NOT to do those things today.

Continue by explaining the *imagine* part. Tell students that they should picture in their mind whatever they are going to do; in this case, write a story entitled "Moving to the Moon." This will help them to focus and loosen up ideas that are creative and imaginative.

Give students an idea of how the entire process works by modeling the three parts of Get Ready. You can do this by saying something like this:

Teacher: I'm going to try out the Get Ready step of the Mental Management Strategy and see what happens. First, I'm going to close my eyes and try to clear my mind of everything. *(Pause for a few seconds.)*

Now I am going to remember. I'm going to think back to the last time that I wrote a story. I remember that I just took off and started writing about anything that came into my head. I didn't think about it much and the story wasn't very interesting or clever. So today I'll remember NOT to do that. I'll take more time to think about what I want to write and I'll spend more time imagining. *(Pause.)*

I'm imagining my trip to the moon and the moment the door of the spacecraft opens. Now I can feel a strong mixture of fear and excitement as I meet the moon creatures for the first time. I'm trying to focus a picture in my mind of exactly what the moon creatures look like. *(Pause.)* And how they act when they meet me.

Now the scene changes and I'm walking away from the spacecraft. I look around and pay attention to where I am and what's around me. We get into a shuttle. *(Pause.)*

Suggest that students try out this step themselves. Remind them to pause, to remember, and to imagine.

3. Invite students to try their hand at doing the task.

After students have had sufficient time to get ready, give them time to actually begin to write a story entitled "Moving to the Moon." Interrupt students after about twenty minutes and go on with the post-task steps. If you wish to have students complete their stories, suggest another time for them to do so.

4. Explain Make Connections, the first post-task step.

Explain that even though students may not have completed their stories, you want them to get an idea of the two steps they can use AFTER a task is completed. Tell students that they can make any task or learning experience more meaningful and memorable if they make connections.

Ask, "What other things that you do or know about did your story of moving to the moon make you think about? What BIG ideas did it give you?" (Possible answers: *Mine made me think about how we'll have to find a new place to live if we keep ruining our own world, so I guess the BIG idea is ecology and pollution; I thought about friends and friendship because I'd be sad to leave my friends on Earth; I made a connection to Science class because we learned how animals have to adapt to different environments and people have to adapt, too. We'd have to get used to wearing different clothes, eating different food, and figuring out new ways to do things on the Moon.*)

Compliment students on their responses. Then help them stretch their thinking by suggesting that they make a connection between their story and Math, or between their story and fairness. Encourage everyone to think about it and to discuss their ideas with each other. Turn away and do something else for a few moments to give them time to think.

Then ask, "Can anyone make a connection to Math or to fairness?" (A possible answer for Math: *A connection to math could be that, in my story at least, the people had to know a lot about math and machines to get to the moon in the first place and to live there.* A possible answer for fairness: *Well, I think a connection to fairness would be who could go to the moon and who couldn't go if the Earth was a mess and everyone wanted to leave.*)

If time permits, challenge students to make connections between writing a story and doing other tasks. (Possible answers: *In Social Studies, imagining what people are like in other countries; in spelling tests, thinking about how to spell words such as "Martian."*)

5. Present Think About Thinking, the last post-task step.

Direct students' attention to the poster and have someone read the name of this last step and the three related questions. Suggest that students evaluate the effectiveness of their thinking during this lesson by having them do one of the following exercises:

■ Have students pretend that a filmmaker captured their thoughts on film as they were working. Now they can replay their thoughts and see what they thought about, where their thinking was good or easy, and where it was not focused or difficult.

■ Have students pretend that Jiminy Cricket has been listening to their thoughts and imagine what he would say about them. How would he answer the questions: What went well? What didn't go well? What could be improved?

Give students a few minutes to reflect and then invite them to share their evaluations of their thought processes with the class. As students offer their evaluations, acknowledge their efforts and encourage them to analyze their comments. Your classroom discussion might sound something like this:

Student: It was hard for me to think of an idea. I didn't like the topic.

Teacher: Okay, what could you do next time to help solve this problem?

Student: I guess I could have figured out how to make something up so I'd like it, or I could have asked you if I could write about something else.

Teacher: Those are two good ideas. Was anything hard for anyone else?

Student: It was hard for me to write neatly. I thought we had to hand the story in, so I worried about it being neat.

Teacher: Can you think of a few ways to handle the neatness problem next time?

Student: Well, I could have asked you ahead of time if the papers had to be handed in. Also, I could spend more time getting ready by thinking before I wrote anything down. Then I wouldn't have to erase so much.

6. Review the Mental Management Strategy.

End the lesson by complimenting students on their work. Then direct attention to the poster again as you quickly summarize the main steps in this strategy. You might do this by saying something like, "You did great! You prepared yourself well to do some creative writing in Get Ready, the pre-task step. After you finished writing, you used two post-task steps. In the Make Connections step, you connected the writing task to other things you know about in order to make your knowledge more meaningful and memorable. In the Think About Thinking step, you evaluated your own thought processes and came up with some great ways to improve your thinking AND your writing in the future. The Mental Management Strategy CAN help you become better thinkers, able to more intelligently use your minds. Congratulations!"

Note: An alternate Orientation Lesson begins on the next page. See page 12 for the Classroom Guide and the remainder of the Orientation Lesson materials.

The Memorizing Lesson

1. Direct attention to the poster.

Read the title of the poster: The Mental Management Strategy. Ask a volunteer to tell what the word *strategy* means. (Possible answer: *A plan or method or series of steps used to reach a particular goal or result.*) If necessary, offer the clue that a strategy is a necessary step in sports such as football and in military operations. Have students read the poster copy.

Point out that the things listed on the poster tell about certain actions that anyone can take to make thinking more meaningful and memorable. The actions in thinking are a lot like playing a sport because you get better at it if you plan what to do, then practice doing it.

Ask, "When might you do a better job of thinking?" (Possible answers: *In reading, so I understand as I go along; in studying, so that I remember later on; in writing stories, so I get better ideas before I write; in thinking about how something I learned in class can be useful some other time;* and so on.)

Tell students that what they just named are all thinking situations. Explain that the Mental Management Strategy will help them by providing a method or plan to use before they do something in order to proceed wisely and avoid problems. It will also help them to analyze success or failure after the task is done in order to improve their performance.

Ask, "Why do you think the authors selected a sandwich as a comparison for this strategy?" (Possible answer: *One slice of bread is like the first step in planning, the filling is like the thinking task, and the other slice of bread is like what you do after the thinking task. They all go together.*)

2. Explain the Get Ready step.

Tell students that they will be using the Mental Management Strategy to help them memorize the Preamble to the Constitution. They will begin by doing the pre-task step called *Get Ready.*

Say something like, "You can see from the poster that the first step you should take before you begin the task is to get ready for it. The Get Ready step has three parts: pause, remember, and imagine. *Pause* means to stop briefly. During that time, you clear your minds in order to concentrate on the task you are about to begin. You can close your eyes or put your head on your desk if it will help you concentrate."

Explain that *remember* means to think back to the last time you did a similar task, in this case memorize something, and think about how you can do it even better this time. Ask questions like the following to help students do this.

Ask, "What did you do the last time you memorized something that was really good or helpful?" Accept and record students' answers on the board or chart. Suggest that they remember to repeat these actions today.

Then ask, "What did you do the last time that didn't work or that made the task harder?" Again, accept and record answers. Remind students NOT to do those things today.

Continue by explaining the *imagine* part. Tell students that they should picture in their mind whatever they are going to do; in this case, memorize a paragraph of an historical document. This will help them to focus and loosen up ideas that are creative and imaginative.

Give students an idea of how the entire process works by modeling the three parts of Get Ready. You can do this by saying something like this:

Teacher: I'm going to try out the Get Ready step of the Mental Management Strategy and see what happens. First, I'm going to close my eyes and try to clear my mind of everything. *(Pause for a few seconds.)*

Now I am going to remember. I'm going to think back to the last time I tried to memorize something. It was last night when I was preparing this lesson. I remember that I skipped over the word *preamble* and didn't look up the definition. I had a general idea of what it meant, but really wasn't sure. I will NOT do that today. Instead, I will look up words I don't know in a dictionary to be sure of their meanings.

I'll also spend some time imagining. I will picture in my mind everything I can about the Preamble to the Constitution. This will help me focus on what I am going to memorize. *(Pause.)*

I'm getting a mental picture of the men who wrote the Constitution. I can picture George Washington, James Madison, Benjamin Franklin and others—all wearing powdered wigs. *(Pause.)*

Now the scene changes and I see the National Archives in Washington, DC, where the original document is kept. It looks so beautiful and the handwriting is so different than ours is now. *(Pause.)*

Now I think back to what I read about the war with England for our independence as a country and I get another picture in my mind. *(Pause.)* The year—it is 1787.

Suggest that students try out this step themselves. Ask them to sit quietly for a few minutes to get ready to memorize the Preamble to the Constitution. Remind them to pause, to remember, and to imagine.

3. Invite students to try their hand at doing the task.

After students have had sufficient time to get ready, pass out copies of the Preamble. Invite them to begin memorizing this paragraph. Interrupt students after about twenty minutes and go on with the post-task steps. If you wish to have students check their memorization, suggest that they recite the Preamble to a partner at the end of this lesson.

4. Explain Make Connections, the first post-task step.

Explain that even though students may not have completed their memorizations, you want them to get an idea of the two steps they can use AFTER a task is completed. Tell students that they can make any task or learning experience more meaningful and memorable if they make connections.

Ask, "What other things does the Preamble to the Constitution make you think about? What BIG ideas does it give you?" (Possible answers: *It makes me think about how hard to read most official papers are and that the language is impossible to understand; it makes me wonder what other countries' Constitutions are like, or if they even have them. I wonder if Russia has a Constitution. Also, wouldn't every country want justice? I thought of writing introductions or beginning paragraphs because you have to make them interesting or no one will want to read the rest.*)

Compliment students on their responses. Then help them stretch their thinking by suggesting that they make a connection between the Preamble and Art, or between the Preamble and progress. Encourage everyone to think about it and discuss their ideas with each other. Turn away and do something else for a few moments to give them time to think.

Then ask, "Can anyone make a connection to Art or to progress?" (A possible answer for Art: *It's easy to connect it to art because it's written artistically, or poetically. I think that's why people like it. It's beautiful in its own way.* A possible answer for progress: *It makes me think about progress because people were trying to make a better government, to make progress. That made me also think that progress is slow—establishing justice and promoting the general welfare and all are hard to do, but we keep trying. I guess that's progress.*)

If time permits, challenge students to make connections between memorizing the Preamble and doing other tasks. (Possible answers: *Going to the store and remembering to get some things and forgetting others; listening to politicians' speeches on TV and feeling that they sound good but you're not sure what they really mean.*)

5. Present Think About Thinking, the last post-task step.

Direct students' attention to the poster and have someone read the name of this last step and the three related questions. Suggest that students evaluate the effectiveness of their thinking during this lesson by having them do one of the following exercises:

- Have students pretend that a filmmaker captured their thoughts on film as they were working. Now they can replay their thoughts and see what they thought about, where their thinking was good or easy, and where it was not focused or difficult.

- Have students pretend that Jiminy Cricket has been listening to their thoughts and imagine what he would say about them. How would he answer the questions: What went well? What didn't go well? What could be improved?

Give students a few minutes to reflect and then invite them to share their evaluations of their thought processes with the class. As students offer their evaluations, acknowledge their efforts and encourage them to analyze their comments. Your classroom discussion might sound something like this:

Student: I worked with Jenny. We didn't know the meaning of some words so we used two dictionaries, and each of us looked up different words. It went fast and it helped.

Teacher: Good idea. Who else has an observation?

Student: Not very much went well for me. It was really hard.

Teacher: All right. What was hard?

Student: It was hard to understand and really hard to memorize.

Teacher: Can you be more specific? WHAT exactly was hard to understand, and WHY was it hard to memorize?

Student: Well, I didn't know the meanings of lots of words, and so I looked them all up. Then, I got mixed up about what meant what when I went back to read the Preamble. There were so many words!

Teacher: What do you think you could do next time to solve that problem?

Student: Some people wrote down the hard words on paper. After they looked up the definitions, they wrote in their own words what each word meant. I could have done that.

Teacher: Good solution. Now what about memorizing? What was hard about that?

Student: I couldn't remember it! I'd start at the beginning, and by the time I got to the end, I couldn't remember the beginning.

Teacher: What do you think you could do differently the next time you try to memorize something?

Student: I think I should just try to remember little parts instead of trying to memorize the whole thing at once.

6. Review the Mental Management Strategy.

End the lesson by complimenting students on their work. Then direct attention to the poster again as you quickly summarize the main steps in this strategy. You might do this by saying something like, "You did great! You prepared yourself well to tackle the Preamble to the Constitution in Get Ready, the pre-task step. After you finished memorizing, you used two post-task steps. In the Make Connections step, you connected memorizing the Preamble to other things you know about in order to make your knowledge more meaningful and memorable. In the Think About Thinking step, you evaluated your own thought processes and came up with some great ways to improve your thinking AND memorizing in the future. The Mental Management Strategy CAN help you become better thinkers, able to more intelligently use your minds. Congratulations!"

Classroom Guide

1. Direct attention to the poster.

Call attention to the name of the strategy: Mental Management. Discuss the sandwich image and invite students to express why they think this image was used to representthis strategy.

2. Explain the Get Ready step.

Tell students what task they will be doing (either writing a story about moving to the moon or memorizing the Preamble to the Constitution). Present the three parts to this step: pause, remember, and imagine. Model each of these parts, then ask students to do them.

3. Invite students to try their hand at doing the task.

Conduct this part of the lesson as you normally would by having students work alone, work in groups, or work with partners to either write or memorize.

4. Explain Make Connections, the first post-task step.

To prompt connections to other knowledge or experiences, ask questions such as: "What other things did this task (writing about moving to the moon or memorizing the Preamble to the Constitution) make you think about?" and "What BIG ideas did it give you?"

5. Present Think About Thinking, the last post-task step.

Encourage students to analyze the process that they have just completed. Ask questions such as: "What went well?" "What was hard?" and "What can be improved the next time?"

6. Review the Mental Management Strategy.

Conclude by complimenting students on their work. Using the poster, quickly summarize what they have done.

After-the-Lesson Checklist

■ Did you adequately explain the purpose of this strategy?

■ Did your students seem to understand how to use the steps?

■ Did you give students enough time to think?

■ Did you keep the lesson moving and wrap it up within about 40 minutes?

Teachers' Questions and Authors' Answers

Q: Will my students be able to and want to learn this new strategy?

A: We believe that all students can learn to be better critical, creative, and reflective thinkers. We have worked with hundreds of students of different ages, at different ability levels, and in various settings. All were able to do this work and most students really enjoyed it. In fact, you may find that many students, some who traditionally do poorly in school, prefer this open kind of process to the traditional "right answer" kind of classroom activity.

Don't worry. Your students will not refuse to offer ideas and responses, although you may have to give them time and encouragement. Students need to develop trust that you and the other students won't laugh at their ideas—especially their creative ones. Students will enjoy doing this if you make sure that the atmosphere is friendly and inviting.

Q: Asking students open-ended questions that have no right answers and recording whatever they say makes me feel as if my classroom is out of my control. How can I feel less awkward about this?

A: The feelings you have are understandable. Sometimes changing the way you do something is uncomfortable at first. However, if you stick with it, things will get better and easier.

The first challenge is to make the decision that you will work with students on improving their thinking abilities. Then spend the time to make sure that you create a "thinking classroom." A thinking classroom is a place where students are encouraged to come up with their own ideas, share them with others, talk about them and sometimes challenge other ideas and debate issues.

At first, such a classroom may feel chaotic to you, but keep in mind that you are still the teacher and the manager of your classroom. The thinking classroom, just like any other classroom, has rules that you, perhaps along with your students, establish. It is important that classroom interactions are well managed by you. Activities that encourage students to think do not necessarily rely on you to have all the answers, but you do need to be a strong facilitator. Let us assure you that the more often you do this, the more comfortable you will feel.

GET READY *Concentrated Practices*

Purpose of these Practices

Students now have a general idea of how the Mental Management Strategy works. During yesterday's Orientation Lesson, students overviewed all three steps of the process. During the next four days they will concentrate on mastering the first step.

Most people plunge into a thinking task without taking the time necessary to prepare a proper frame of mind. Practicing the Get Ready step will prompt students to get into a focused and fertile state of mind in order to do their best thinking.

Preparation

- Display the Mental Management poster in a prominent place in the classroom.

- Read through the Classroom Guide on the next page.

- Identify seven places in your curriculum for the remaining four days of the week in which students can practice this step. (For these brief practices, once in the morning and once in the afternoon is desirable.) Record these subjects and tasks in the Weekly Planner on page 37. Some possibilities are:

Reading	Get ready to read a story silently.
Mathematics	Get ready to take a quiz.
Art	Get ready to work on a group project.
Language Arts	Get ready to write a report.
Social Studies	Get ready to discuss a current event.
Science	Get ready to carry out an experiment.
General	Get ready to watch an educational telecast.

  (See page 42 for additional suggestions.)

- Use the Working Outline on page 38 to make notes, recommendations, or changes in your daily lesson plans.

Approximate Classroom Time Needed

WEEK 1   Tuesday: *10 minutes*
          Wednesday – Friday: *2 minutes twice a day*

Classroom Guide

1. Call attention to the poster.

Focus attention on the Get Ready step. Help students recall the three parts of this step: pause, remember, and imagine.

Then explain that for the rest of this week they will only practice the Get Ready step in order to understand it well enough to use on their own in any thinking situation. Tell students that today they will practice this step as they get ready to (*name the task for today*).

2. Ask students to pause.

Encourage all to relax and clear their minds by closing their eyes or putting their heads down. Suggest that they take fifteen seconds to breath deeply and focus their thoughts on the task at hand.

3. Ask students to remember.

Ask students to think about the last time that they did a similar task. Encourage them to reflect on WHAT went well and to remember WHY it went well. (*Pause.*) Suggest that students remember to follow those actions today. Then ask them to remember if anything went wrong and why it went wrong. (*Pause.*) Remind them NOT to do these things today.

4. Ask students to imagine.

Suggest that they create vivid pictures in their mind about the topic they are using. If students are working alone or in groups, tell them to begin only when they have a good mental image of their topic. If students will work as a class on a task, such as taking a quiz, proceed to give the quiz after students have spent a few minutes imagining.

As students become more comfortable with the Get Ready step in the next practice sessions, minimize your guidance. At the most, simply remind students to pause, remember, and imagine. Then give them time to do so.

5. Conclude the practice.

Praise students for their efforts and briefly review what they have done in this practice and why. Encourage them to use these steps as they prepare to do other learning tasks today.

A Classroom Example

You have decided to use this step before students begin a writing project. Your lesson for this practice might develop something like this:

Teacher: Before you begin writing your story, let's take a minute as a class to do the Get Ready step. Look at the poster. What are the three parts to this step?

Student: Pause, remember, and imagine.

Teacher: Right. Now let's do what the words suggest. First, everyone pause to clear your minds. Close your eyes if you want, take a deep breath and just relax for a moment. Let your mind clear. Don't think about anything at all.

The teacher gives students about 15 seconds of silence to clear their minds and models the step by doing it also.

Teacher: Okay, now everyone do the next part of the step—remember. Think back to the last time you wrote a story. What about it did you struggle with and how can you do better this time? Remind yourself to work hard on the problems you had the last time.

The teacher mentions a few problems that many of the students shared in their previous writing assignments.

Student: I had trouble with grammar so I should try to do better and check over my work and look for errors this time.

To save time and make this a quiet, individual step, the teacher thanks the student and then continues.

Teacher: Everybody please put your hands down. Just do this step in your heads, okay? That way you won't be distracted by other people talking. You can prepare yourself for the task. Everybody please take a few moments to remember.

As students spend these moments remembering, the teacher also takes about 15 seconds of silence to do so.

Teacher: Now, everyone should imagine. Think about the topic of your story. Who will the characters be? What do they look like? Where are they? What will they do? Get a good mental picture of your story. Try to imagine it. When you are ready, begin writing.

Students take a few seconds longer to imagine their story, then open their eyes and get to work on their stories.

After-the Lesson Checklist

■ Did students understand the purpose of this step? If not, could you do more modeling in the next practice?

■ Did you allow sufficient quiet time to think?

■ Did you limit the lesson time to a few minutes?

■ Did you "get ready" for this practice, clearing and focusing your own mind?

Teachers' Questions and Authors' Answers

Q: How do I know that my students are really carrying out the Get Ready step if they do it silently in their heads?

A: Get Ready is indeed a difficult step to monitor and to evaluate. One way you can determine whether your students have the right idea or not is to have one student do the remember or the imagine step out loud for the class. You can also have volunteers share the ideas they came up with for each step. Use these suggestions only the first few times to ensure that everyone knows what to do. For those who continue to have difficulty with this step later on, you can give three quiet prompts: pause, remember, imagine.

An important outcome of this activity is that it teaches students to be in control of their own thinking without interference. Another reason to keep the Get Ready step silent and personal is to minimize the time. You will find that doing this step out loud takes five or more minutes; doing it silently takes less than one minute.

MAKE CONNECTIONS *Concentrated Practices*

Purpose of these Practices

Make Connections is a transfer step designed to help students form new ways of thinking about something by connecting it to knowledge and information they already have. By creating a web of connections, students can make what they learn more meaningful and memorable. Along with the next step, Think About Thinking, this step helps you and your students conclude a lesson or an activity in a way that highlights its relevance. Students are left with the BIG ideas they came up with through their thinking.

Preparation

- Display the Mental Management poster in a prominent place in the classroom.

- Read through the Classroom Guide on the next page.

- Identify five places in your curriculum for the upcoming week in which students can practice this step. Record these subjects and tasks in the Weekly Planner on page 37. Some possibilities are:

Spelling	Make connections after students have completed the first days' written work.
Language Arts	Make connections after students have learned a new part of speech.
Reading	Make connections after students have read a nonfictional story.

(See page 42 for additional suggestions.)

- In order to challenge your students' thinking skills, write two or three questions on the Working Outline on page 39 to prompt students to connect what they already know with the task they have just completed. Here are a few examples of the kinds of questions you could ask:

What do spelling patterns have to do with history? art?

What else do spelling patterns remind you of?

Does this part of speech remind you of anything in science? travel?

How do the events in the story connect to Mathematics?

What other things did the story make you think of?

Approximate Classroom Time Needed

WEEK 2   Monday: *20 minutes*

Tuesday – Friday: *15 minutes each day*

Classroom Guide

1. After students finish a task, call attention to the poster.

Have a volunteer summarize the information on the poster, then focus attention on the second step: Make Connections. Review the concept of connecting new knowledge to what they already know. Be sure to explain that the point of making connections is to make what they learn more meaningful, memorable, and useful to them.

2. Ask students to make some connections.

Ask general prompt questions, such as: What does (*this task or topic*) remind you of? What other things like this do you know about? What other school subjects can you connect this to?

Be patient. Give students sufficient time to think, to mull over ideas, and to come up with connections.

3. Ask students to respond.

Acknowledge each oral response by nodding or by saying, "Okay" or "Yes" in quick verbal confirmation. Do not offer any evaluation of the responses. You might briefly record the responses, thus giving students more time to think.

4. When students run out of ideas, use prompt questions again.

Prompt questions can spark thinking when ideas are not flowing. They can also demonstrate how students themselves can pose questions on their own. Use repetitive wordings, such as: What other things does (*this task or topic*) remind you of? What other things like this do you know about? Can you connect this to other things that you are studying?

Once again, give students time to think. Then ask for additional responses. Challenge students to make other connections by suggesting new and perhaps unusual categories that have not been mentioned.

5. Conclude the practice.

Congratulate students on their hard work. Remind them of the importance of doing this type of thinking as they learn new things and undertake new tasks. Reinforce the point that making connections will help them do new tasks and make learning more meaningful to them.

A Classroom Example

Your lesson includes viewing a film about Helen Keller (the task and topic). Your practice for this lesson might develop something like this:

Teacher: Now that the film is over, let's make some connections to other things we know. What did this film remind you of?

Not one hand goes up. The silence is awkward, but the teacher calmly waits. Students understand this step, but they find it a bit difficult. The teacher softly repeats the question and turns away, attending to the movie projector to give them time to think. Finally, one or two hands go up.

Student: It reminds me of kids who can see but can't read. They have a handicap, too. It just isn't visible.

The teacher nods and calls on another student.

Student: Helen Keller reminded me of a pig when she went around grabbing food off everyone else's plate!

The teacher looks at the student, but doesn't react to the comment. Instead, the teacher calls on another student.

Student: It made me think about how sign language is a language just like any other one. I know that sounds dumb, but I never thought of it that way before.

Teacher: Sometimes we surprise ourselves when we come up with a connection that seems so obvious, but we never thought of it before.

Student: My connection has to do with laws. Laws say that everyone, even people with handicaps, have to be educated. They can't just be left to run wild like Helen did at first.

No more students are willing to offer their thoughts. After a few moments of silence, the teacher decides to use a prepared prompt question to jog their thinking.

Teacher: Okay. Well, think about this. How does the story of Helen Keller remind you of human nature? Who can make a connection here?

Student: I know. It seems like human nature to be afraid of or mean to people like Helen Keller at first. But if you stop to think about it, it's better and fairer to be nice and try to help people.

Other students respond to the prompt question and after more ideas and some discussion, the teacher concludes the lesson.

After-the-Lesson Checklist

■ Did you integrate the practice into a regularly scheduled lesson with a concrete task or interesting topic?

■ Did you prepare relevant and thoughtful prompt questions?

■ Did you gradually decrease YOUR use of prompts and encourage students to prompt themselves and each other?

- Did you avoid positive or negative reactions to answers?

- However, did you ask students to clarify any answers that seemed inadequate or inappropriate?

- Were you patient, knowing that this can be a hard step?

Teachers' Questions and Authors' Answers

Q: What do I do when my students have no ideas?

A: First of all, make sure that they understand what it is that you are asking them to do. This process is new to most students and making connections can be a difficult step—even when students are familiar with it. The key is using a few good prompt questions. Use familiar wording and repeat questions so students learn to do this themselves.

If you are confident that your students understand this step and you have used a good prompt question, but they still aren't offering ideas, continue to give them thinking time. Do a "turning away" activity, such as erasing the board or arranging papers or books. This will allow thinking time without the added pressure of your gaze.

If students run out of answers before you feel they have really thought hard about it, urge them to focus on thinking of unusual or less obvious connections. You could also set quotas by saying that you'd like a specific number of answers—four, for example. This supplies a concrete goal and students are often likely to rise to the challenge.

Q: Why is strong praise not used when students give interesting answers?

A: Research shows that students notice differences in praise. If they see big differences, they often start focusing on the game of getting the praise instead of on the task. Other students may quietly drop out. Fuller and more honest participation results when strong praise is avoided in favor of mildly positive acceptance of everyone's efforts. Therefore, a simple "Okay," or "Good," or "Yes, that's interesting" is preferred. Recording all responses on the board or on a chart also shows that you acknowledge and appreciate all ideas.

Purpose of these Practices

This step teaches students that thinking is something that can be reviewed and improved upon. By stepping back after a task and reflecting on their thought processes, students empower themselves to be better thinkers.

In this step students will learn to ask themselves three questions: What went well with my thinking? What was hard? What could be improved the next time? Answering these questions will teach students to be aware of how they think, to evaluate strengths and weaknesses, and to plan to think better in the future.

Preparation

- Display the Mental Management poster in a prominent place in the classroom.

- Read through the Classroom Guide on the next page.

- Identify five places in your curriculum for the upcoming week in which students can conclude·a task with this last, post-task step. Record these in the Weekly Planner on page 37. Some possibilities across the curriculum are:

  Think about thinking after a role-play or a skit.

  Think about thinking after a handwriting exercise.

  Think about thinking after making an observation.

  Think about thinking after planning a trip or an event.

  Think about thinking after making a timeline.

  Think about thinking after taking a quiz.

  (See page 42 for additional suggestions.)

- Use the Working Outline on page 40 to make notes, recommendations, or changes in your daily lesson plans.

Approximate Classroom Time Needed

WEEK 3   Monday: *20 minutes*

Tuesday – Friday: *15 minutes each day*

Classroom Guide

1. After students finish a task, call attention to the poster.

Read the three questions in the Think About Thinking step. Quickly review with your students the concept of thinking about their own thought processes. Be sure to explain that the point of this activity is for them to become aware of their own thinking and identify ways to make it better.

Use either the mental movie or the Jiminy Cricket device presented in the Orientation Lesson to help explain what this step is all about. It is important to model this activity by describing your own thought processes so students will get the idea of what they should do.

2. Ask students to think about their thinking.

Allow a few minutes of quiet time to give students a chance to review the thinking they did on the task just completed. While they are thinking, write the three questions for this step on the board or chart, forming columns to record students' responses under each question:

What went well? What was hard? What can be improved?

3. Ask students to respond to each of the three questions.

If responses do not come readily, reflect on your own thinking. Offer a personal example that ties in with the task. For instance, think over your presentation of this lesson. What was easy about conducting this lesson? What was hard to do? What could you do better the next time?

As students come up with their own ideas, write each response under the appropriate question. Remember not to praise or criticize any responses.

4. Conclude the practice.

Congratulate students on their work. Briefly summarize the suggestions for improving thinking and stress the importance of what was done today. Remind students that reflecting on their thinking will give them the power to improve it.

A Classroom Example

Your lesson includes writing an original haiku (the task). Your practice for this lesson might develop something like this:

Teacher: Now that you've finished your poems, take a few minutes to think back to what you were thinking while writing your haiku. To help you remember what your thinking was like, imagine that a movie was made inside your head while you were writing. What would the movie look like? Or imagine that Jiminy Cricket was sitting on your shoulder as you were writing, watching your thoughts. What would he have seen? Take some time now to remember your thinking while you were writing your haiku.

The teacher writes the three questions across the top of the board or chart: What went well? What was hard? What can be improved?

Student: I don't really get what you mean.

Teacher: Here's an example. Thinking back to when I wrote haiku, I remember that at first I concentrated very hard on finding an idea, and that part was hard. After a while, I relaxed and ideas seemed to come more easily.

Student: I know what went well! It was fun to write the poem once I got an idea, but it was hard to get a good idea. At first I could only think of things that seemed dumb.

The teacher writes "Fun, once you get an idea" under the question "What went well?"

Student: For me, the part that was the most fun was reading haiku before we started. I liked the one you read today.

Teacher: Okay, I'll put that under the first question, too.

Student: It was hard to say what I wanted with so few words.

Teacher: All right. I'll put that under "What was hard?"

The teacher records more answers to the first two questions, then suggests that they move on to the third question.

Student: I needed more time. We only had thirty minutes and I didn't finish.

Student: We could read our haiku out loud to test how they sound.

The teacher records these and a few other ideas, then concludes the lesson.

After-the-Lesson Checklist

- Did you give students enough time to think?

- Did you model activities for students?

- Did you wrap the practice up in 20 minutes or less?

- Did you bring closure to significant points and summarize what students said about ways to improve their thinking?

Teachers' Questions and Authors' Answers

Q: Aren't children in elementary school too young to reflect on their thinking in a meaningful way?

A: Research shows that children this age are most definitely able to reflect on their thought processes and talk about them. Without prompt questions, however, children are often not aware of how they are thinking or how they can become more independent thinkers and learners. It is not that children CANNOT think about thinking; it is simply that they DO NOT. Hence, the need to show them how to go about it. By using either the mental movie or the Jiminy Cricket device, you can help children "watch" their own thinking and report on it.

Q: Won't students feel that the practice is incomplete by rambling on about their thinking after the task is over?

A: They might. That's why it is important for you to bring closure to this step by summarizing what students have said and reminding them of the importance of thinking about thinking. All that you really need to do is recap the ideas for improvements that students came up with in answer to the question about what can be improved the next time. This is an effective way to conclude these practices.

Q: I have a concern about asking, "What was hard?" Won't I just get complaints? And if so, should I just write these things on the board without comment?

A: Yes and no. You should write even the complaints on the board. It is important for students to feel that any ideas are acceptable. However, you must ask students to explain why. If a student says something was boring, for example, ask for an explanation of exactly what was boring and why. Ask specific questions like, "Was the whole thing boring, or just a certain part? Which part was boring? What can you or I do in the future to make the activity more interesting?" Remember that the best way to cope with negative answers is to ask for details. Then ask students for solutions.

PULLING IT ALL TOGETHER

Purpose of these Practices

Now that students have had concentrated practice on each of the three steps of Mental Management, it is time to put them all together and practice using the whole strategy. This is an important week. Students will come to understand that good thinking involves an entire process—before, during, and after a task is completed. By the end of the week, they should be on their way to internalizing this process.

Preparation

- Display the Mental Management poster in a prominent place in the classroom.

- Read through the Classroom Guide on the next page.

- Identify five places in your curriculum for the upcoming week in which students can practice this strategy. Think about places where your students will most likely experience success. Record these in the Weekly Planner on page 37. Some possibilities are:

Social Studies	Evaluate the effect of Julius Caesar on history.
Language Arts	Write a political ad or slogan.
Reading	Prepare a book report about a biography.
Math	Work multiplication problems or fractions.
General	Decide on the best time and place to study.

  (See page 42 for additional suggestions.)

- Think through how each lesson might unfold as you encourage students to go through the steps of this strategy: Get Ready before the actual task, then Make Connections and Think About Thinking after the task. Use the Working Outline on page 41 for notes about any modeling, ideas for prompt questions and connections to other subject areas that you might use. Do this for each of the five lessons.

- Have copies of The Mental Management Checklist on page 36 to give to your students.

Approximate Classroom Time Needed

WEEK 4 Monday – Friday: *20 minutes each day*

Classroom Guide

1. Suggest that students use the Mental Management Strategy.

Before students begin the task that you have chosen, suggest that this would be a good opportunity to use the thinking strategy that they have been practicing. If you think it would be helpful, pass out copies of The Mental Management Checklist worksheet.

Remind them to use all of the steps, starting with Get Ready. Call attention to the poster and emphasize the importance of this "thinking sandwich ingredient." Then remind them

- to pause—to relax and clear their minds

- to remember—to think about the last time they did this task, and repeat what worked well and avoid doing what did not work well

- and to imagine—to create a clear picture in their mind that relates to what they are going to do.

2. Have students work on the task.

Direct students to do their work in the usual manner and the usual time allotted.

3. After the task, remind students to do the two post-task steps.

Call attention to the poster again and remind students to make connections— to ask themselves questions, such as: What does this remind me of? What other things that I know about does this relate to? What other school subjects can this be connected to? (If necessary, use prompt questions to facilitate their thinking.)

Finally, remind them to think about their thinking by asking themselves questions, such as: What was easy? What was hard? What can I do better the next time I do this task?

4. Conclude the lesson.

Congratulate students on their successful use of the Mental Management Strategy. Point out how the strategy helped them with their task by preparing their minds before they started and helping them make connections and reflect on their performance after they finished. Encourage everyone to use this strategy often.

A Classroom Example

You have decided that students will use this strategy to take a test on long division. Your lesson might develop something like this:

Teacher: Before I hand out the tests, I'd like to suggest that this is a good time to use the Mental Management Strategy that you've been learning. You know how to begin with Get Ready. Everyone please take several seconds now to pause and clear your minds.

The teacher pauses for a few seconds, lowering his or her head to do this step, too.

Teacher: Now remember: What things do you need to do better this time? Do you need to remember to check your work? Think about the things you DON'T want to do, like working too fast or not concentrating.

After about ten seconds of silence, the teacher asks students to take some time to imagine. After a few seconds more, the teacher gives the test in the usual manner.

Teacher: Don't forget to do the rest of the thinking strategy! What other things that you know about or do does this test remind you of? What connections can you make?

Student: It reminds me of the time I took a spelling test and didn't check my work. I knew how to spell the words, but I didn't check them over and I made some dumb mistakes.

Teacher: Okay, that's a connection to another kind of test. Any other connections?

Student: Division reminds me of sharing because sometimes you have to break something up to share it.

The teacher collects a few more ideas and decides that additional prompts are not necessary.

Teacher: So what about thinking about your thinking. What was easy and what was hard? What could be done better?

Student: The TEST was really hard. I couldn't do some of it.

Teacher: Is there anything you could do about that?

Student: I guess I can study harder next time and make sure that I understand things before the test.

Teacher: Good suggestions, but how can you do that?

Student: I can ask for help...or pay more attention to my homework.

The teacher concludes by summarizing what students said and points out how the strategy helped them with their tests.

After-the-Lesson Checklist

- Did you give students time to get ready?

- Did you prepare prompt questions and use them if they were needed to help students make connections?

- During the Think About Thinking step, did you make sure that students responded to all three questions?

- Did you keep the practice focused and brief?

- Did you wrap things up by praising your students' efforts?

Teachers' Questions and Authors' Answers

Q: Is it really all right to cut off a discussion while students still have their hands up? That seems unfair, and it may undermine my students' enthusiasm for thinking!

A: Your concerns are valid, but there's another side to the matter. You are trying to introduce a process by taking students through a sequence of activities in the classroom. If these activities run over the suggested time or drag on, both you and your students may become discouraged and bored.

You can, however, minimize negative effects that might result from cutting students off. One successful technique that we mentioned earlier is to set limits on the number of responses you will accept. Tell students beforehand and then stick to it. Make it a point to call on different students throughout the practice sessions. Everyone will feel able to participate; at the same time, you can keep things moving.

Q: I can never get through a practice in the amount of time suggested. Are the time estimates wishful thinking or am I doing something wrong?

A: The classroom time suggested for each practice is realistic, and the more you do this, the more efficient you will become. If you find that you are taking much longer, try the approach just recommended for students who have too many answers. Also, try having students work on paper or in groups, especially if they are already engaged in writing or group work. This will cut down on the amount of time you spend calling on students and writing responses on the board. This approach also helps to ensure that everyone stays involved.

Feel free to be creative and adjust things to suit the needs and individual character of your class. You know your students best, so go ahead and make the modifications necessary to ensure that your students get the benefits of using the strategy.

Q: My students are used to knowing what is expected of them and they are oriented to "right" answers. This new way of working seems alien to them. Even when I try to engage students in creative thinking, some say, "Just tell us the answer! Tell us what you want us to say!"

A: You have the difficult job of undoing something that students have learned to do very well. They have learned to feed back to the teacher what the teacher wants. It may take some time to engage students in creative, reflective thinking, but it is possible.

Give your students time to adjust. Engaging in new adventures requires trust. Students may not really believe that you don't have THE right answer in mind or that you will accept ALL responses as right answers. You must convince them that their performance will be judged solely on how creatively, critically, and reflectively they participate.

Q: My students have completed all of the Mental Management Strategy practices. What do I do next?

A: Continue to suggest times or places during students' daily tasks where they can put the thinking strategy that they have learned to work. And keep using the steps of the strategy!

In the weeks ahead, students will learn two new strategies that they can use while doing tasks. Each strategy can be thought of as a different kind of filling in the "Thinking Sandwich." Students will learn how the Mental Management Strategy and the new strategies can either work together or be used separately.

Teacher Resources

Contents and Notes

We, the people of the United States,

in order to form a more perfect Union,

establish justice,

insure domestic tranquillity,

provide for the common defense,

promote the general welfare,

and secure the blessings of liberty

  to ourselves and our posterity,

do ordain and establish this Constitution

  for the United States of America.

The Mental Management Checklist

1. Get Ready

❑ **Pause.** Prepare to concentrate on what you are about to do. Take at least fifteen seconds of quiet time to clear your mind.

❑ **Remember.** Think back to the last time that you did this or something similar. Think about HOW you did it. Think about how you can do it better this time.

❑ **Imagine.** Create some vivid pictures in your mind about what you will be doing or about the topic.

Do the task. The task is

2. Make Connections

❑ Think about OTHER things that this reminds you of. How does it connect to other things you know about? Does it connect to other things you have done? What BIG ideas do you have?

_____

_____

_____

_____

_____

3. Think About Thinking

❑ What went well?_____

_____

_____

❑ What was hard? _____

_____

_____

❑ What can be improved?_____

_____

_____

Weekly Planner: **The Mental Management Strategy**

WEEK 1: ORIENTATION LESSON & GET READY PRACTICES

MONDAY	TUESDAY	WEDNESDAY	THURSDAY	FRIDAY
Orientation Lang Arts: Story writing or Soc Studies: Memorizing	*Get Ready Practices* Subject & Task	*Get Ready Practices* Subject & Task	*Get Ready Practices* Subject & Task	*Get Ready Practices* Subject & Task

WEEK 2: MAKE CONNECTIONS PRACTICES

MONDAY	TUESDAY	WEDNESDAY	THURSDAY	FRIDAY
Subject & Task	Subject & Task	Subject & Task	Subject & Task	Subject & Task

WEEK 3: THINK ABOUT THINKING PRACTICES

MONDAY	TUESDAY	WEDNESDAY	THURSDAY	FRIDAY
Subject & Task	Subject & Task	Subject & Task	Subject & Task	Subject & Task

WEEK 4: PULLING IT ALL TOGETHER

MONDAY	TUESDAY	WEDNESDAY	THURSDAY	FRIDAY
Subject & Task	Subject & Task	Subject & Task	Subject & Task	Subject & Task

Working Outline: **Get Ready**

1. Call attention to the poster and the three parts of the Get Ready step—pause, remember, and imagine.

2. Ask students to pause and focus their thoughts.

3. Ask students to remember how they did a task like this before. Ask: What went well and why? What went wrong and why? How can you do this better?

4. Ask students to imagine by creating vivid pictures in their minds about the topic or task at hand.

5. Conclude with praise and a brief review or summary .

Working Outline: **Make Connections**

1. After student finish a task, call attention to the poster and the Make Connections step.

2. Ask students to make connections to other things that they know about or other school subjects. Use prompt questions to help. (Give them time to think!)

3. Ask students to respond and accept all answers without judgment. Record responses if you think it will help them focus and think. If necessary, use more prompt questions. (Be patient!)

4. Conclude with praise, encouragement, and a brief review.

Working Outline: **Think About Thinking**

1. After students have finished a task, call attention to the poster and this final step. Explain the mental movie or the Jiminy Cricket devices to help them think about their thinking.

2. Invite students to think about their thinking. Ask: What was easy? What was hard? What can be improved?

3. Encourage students to respond to each of the three questions. Accept all answers. If needed, help clarify responses and record them.

4. Conclude with praise, encouragement, and a brief review.

1. Suggest that students use the Mental Management Strategy before a specific task. Have them use the Mental Management Checklist to guide them through the process. Remind them to Get Ready—to pause, remember, and imagine.

2. Have everyone do the task as usual.

3. After the task, remind students to make connections. Ask: What does this remind you of? What other things or subjects do you know about that you can connect this to? Use more prompt questions if necessary.

4. Then encourage them to think about their thinking. Ask: What was easy? What was hard? What can you do better? Use more prompt questions if necessary.

5. Conclude with praise and a brief review.

Opportunities in Your Daily Curriculum

The Mental Management Strategy can be applied to almost any academic task or topic and many common events in your daily classroom life. The list below offers some suggestions for places in the curriculum where you might infuse an isolated step (Get Ready, Make Connections, Think About Thinking) or the whole strategy. You will find that you have many more ideas that are specific to your classes. Expand and adapt this list for future use. Be sure to share and exchange your ideas with other teachers.

Language Arts
creative writing
editing
proofreading
reading aloud
writing a book report
writing an invitation
learning correct usage
persuasive writing

Mathematics
equations
area
fractions
mixed fractions
geometry
problem solving
memorizing

Social Studies
the continents
capital cities
war
trial by jury
nuclear testing
sharecropping
maps and globes
transportation
The Civil War
peoples of America
industrialization
The Colonies
inventions
presidents

Science and Health
blood types
diseases
the planets
classifying plants
natural resources
clouds
fossils
primates

Music and Art
composers
ballads
quartets
vocalists
Primitive art
Pop art
sketching

General
solving problems
listening
taking notes
studying
taking a test
memorizing
learning something new
creating something
playing a sport
settling an argument
preparing a report
giving a presentation
discussing
persuading

Get Ready Step

Students don't seem to pause. It often helps to have students quiet down, close their eyes, take a deep breath, or put their heads on their desks for a minute.

Students don't seem to remember. If you're not sure whether students are really doing this, do it out loud. Give a few recommendations for what they might think about, what they might do better this time, or ask them for ideas.

Students don't seem to imagine. You can help them begin by verbally describing the task you are about to do or the topic you are about to explore. You could also ask for words that come to mind when they think about the task or topic.

Make Connections Step

Students have trouble making connections. Because this is something new, many students may perceive this step as hard to do. First and foremost, be patient. As awkward as the silences may be, wait for answers. Research shows that even a three-second pause can result in an increase in student responses. Count to ten or walk around the room—do whatever you need to do to give your students time to think and formulate a response. And don't worry about collecting a lot of ideas for this step. One big idea is all that is necessary, although more is great if there is time.

If responses or ideas are still not forthcoming after a period of silence, give prompts to stimulate thinking. Look around your classroom or think about specific examples from your daily curriculum for cues and ideas. Use these as prompts and ask direct questions related to them, such as: What does this have to do with fairness? How does this relate to what we studied yesterday? Does this task (or topic) remind you of anything else we did today?

Giving quotas for answers often helps, too. Ask for a specific number of ideas (at least three or five, for example) and you are very likely to get them.

Think About Thinking Step

Students don't seem to understand this step. The most powerful way for you to convey the point of this step is by modeling it. Think back to when you were preparing this lesson and review aloud for them how it went. It might sound something like this: "Well, I knew that we were going to do this today, and I thought it might be a good task to use but that I had better test it out first. So I started with Get Ready, but I hurried through it, not really giving myself time to clear my mind and focus my attention. I will have to do this better next time. Then I thought back to the last time we did this and I got a good, clear picture of it in my mind. As I imagined doing it again today, I thought that I needed to give everyone as much time as possible, because last time some did not finish." Once students see how it is done and how it helps you think and work better, they are likely to pick up on it themselves.

You can also try to find a metaphor that works for your students. We have used the make-a-movie-about-your-thinking and the Jiminy Cricket ideas, but you or your students may have a better one. As long as it encourages students to review and critique their thinking, try it out. For example, you could use a coaching analogy, explaining that students can be both the coach and the athlete when it comes to thinking skills. Just as a runner can improve his or her performance by taking suggestions from a coach on how to make changes in pacing or breathing, they can make suggestions for improving their thinking skills. Or ask students what improvements they would suggest in their own thinking if they were the teacher.

You might also break the strategy into steps and ask students to describe their thinking at each step: clear, messy, confused, quick, exhausting, fun, and so on. Helping them find words to describe the different steps will help them identify the easy and hard parts, as well as areas for improvement.

In General

The strategy takes too long. The time estimates at the beginning of each practice session are realistic. If you find that you are taking much longer, there are several things you can do. First, try the same approach recommended for situations in which students have too many answers. Set limits on the number of responses you will take and stick to them. Call on different students throughout the session (rather than all with hands up after each question) to keep everyone involved.

Second, try having students work on paper or in groups. This will cut down on the amount of time that you spend calling on students and writing their responses on the board. This will also ensure that everyone stays involved.

If all else fails, you can always trim a lesson down. For example, it is better to do just one or two of the steps thoroughly than to do nothing at all because of time constraints. Use your best judgment about what to leave in and what to leave out. You know what your students need to work on most.

Students give inappropriate answers to questions. Because one purpose of the strategy is to cultivate creative thinking, try not to react at all to silly or unsuitable responses. Write them on the board as you would any other response. By not reacting negatively, you will be allowing students to feel free to take chances with answers or ideas and you may be surprised to find that sometimes the "silly" response generates a good idea. In addition, inappropriate responses will not get anticipated attention. The exception, of course, is genuine discipline problems which you should deal with as usual.

2 | *The Decision-Making Strategy*

Module Two: *Overview*

Module Two teaches students how to think through their own decisions and evaluate decisions that other people have made. Students become involved in searching for thorough and thoughtful answers to three very powerful questions:

1. What are the options?
2. What are the reasons?
3. What is the best choice?

To help students answer each of these questions, specific suggestions called "yardsticks" are used. The yardsticks offer direction or suggestions about what sorts of things students should be thinking about. They also offer criteria by which the quality of thinking can be assessed by the teacher, as well as by the students themselves.

The Decision-Making Strategy can be used as a strategy of its own or it can be infused into the daily classroom curriculum as well as other activities. The strategy can also become a "filler" for the Thinking Sandwich. For example, you might begin a lesson with the pre-task step (Get Ready), then use the Decision-Making Strategy, and conclude with the two post-task steps (Make Connections and Think About Thinking). Combining the two strategies will strengthen students' use of the Mental Management Strategy, enhance their thinking during the Decision-Making Strategy, and enrich their thinking after completing the task (making the decision).

In order that both teachers and students become familiar with the Decision-Making Strategy, it is suggested that some time almost every day be used to present and practice the strategy for a period of four weeks as outlined below.

Suggested Timetable for Module Two

WEEK 5 Monday: **Orientation Lesson** (40 minutes)
Tuesday – Friday: **What Are the Options? Practice**
(20 minutes each day)

WEEK 6 Monday: **What Are the Reasons? Practice** (40 minutes)
Tuesday – Friday: **Practice** (20 minutes each day)

WEEK 7 Any three days: **What is the Best Choice? Practice**
(20 minutes each day)

WEEK 8 Any three days: **Pulling It All Together Practice**
(45 minutes each day)

ORIENTATION LESSON

Purpose of this Lesson

The Orientation Lesson will give students a general understanding of how the Decision-Making Strategy works from beginning to end. It will provide them with a basis upon which they can fine-tune the details of this important strategy over the next four weeks. Learning and practicing this strategy will enable students to become careful and critical decision-makers now and throughout their lives.

Along with the daily decisions of their own lives, students will learn to think about and examine decisions made by others, including historical figures and fictional characters. Although students cannot change decisions made by others, they can gain a deeper understanding of those decisions and the factors that contributed to them, as well as what the consequences might have been if other decisions had been made. Students will also have opportunities to imagine themselves in various situations in which they are asked to recommend careful decisions.

Preparation

- A sample Orientation Lesson is provided on the following pages as a model for your use. Read through it to familiarize yourself with the procedures and the key words and phrases used in this strategy. While many of you will find the topic, child labor laws, to be a useful one to explore with students, some may prefer to choose another topic from their curriculum. (See page 84 for suggestions of other appropriate subject areas and topics.)

- The Classroom Guide on page 53 provides an abbreviated lesson plan which you may find useful in reviewing your lesson strategy and conducting your lesson.

- Display the Decision-Making poster in a prominent place in the classroom.

- All lesson plans in this manual assume that chalkboard and chalk or chart paper and a marker are available to record student responses.

Approximate Classroom Time Needed

WEEK 5 Monday: *40 minutes*

The Children and Jobs Lesson

1. Direct attention to the poster.

Briefly review what strategies are and why they are important to us. Help students recall the previous strategy, Mental Management, that they have learned. Then ask a volunteer to read the name of the new strategy as shown on the poster.

Ask, "Can anyone think of a time outside of the classroom when you have had to make a decision? Briefly tell us about it." (Possible answers: *When I'm deciding what to wear in the morning or what I need to take to school; deciding what I'm going to do after school; deciding how to deal with a brother or sister when we have an argument; deciding what movie I want to see; deciding whether I should do something I really shouldn't; deciding when to get homework done.*)

Then ask students to name times when adults have to make important decisions. (Possible answers: *Whether or not they should go to college; whether or not they will marry someone; which candidate to vote for in an election; whether or not to apply for or accept a job.*)

Continue by asking, "Why do you think it's important to do a good job of thinking through decisions that we have to make?" Accept all answers, then summarize by stressing that not making the best choice or making mistakes often results from not having properly thought through a decision.

2. Present the decision point for students to consider.

Tell students that you want them to decide whether or not children under 14 years of age should be allowed by law to work for pay. Provide students with some background information about child labor in the United States. You can do this by presenting the following facts:

- In colonial times, young children were important laborers in homes as well as outside the home. They were often paid for their work.

- Both boys and girls often worked on farms rather than attend school.

- In the early nineteenth century, girls were employed in textile mills to operate the machines.

- By the end of the nineteenth century, hundreds of thousands of children worked in factories and in mines. Many were injured in accidents or died from diseases related to their jobs.

- In 1938 *The Fair Labor Standards Act*, also known as *The Wages and Hours Act*, became the basic child labor law in the United States. It bans employers engaged in interstate commerce from hiring workers under the ages of 16 or 18 in hazardous occupations. It states that children

14 to 16 years of age may be employed after school hours under certain circumstances. It also says that each state has the power to further control child labor as long as its legislation does not conflict with the federal law.

■ This Act is still the federal law today. However, it now limits the number of hours that children may work during the school year to a total of eighteen hours per week. The Act also restricts children from doing certain types of work, such as mining, meat slicing, poultry and fish processing, and some farming jobs. Punishment for employers who break this law is also clarified.

On the board or chart paper, write: *Decision Point: Whether or not children under 14 years of age should be allowed by law to work for pay.* Suggest that students take a minute or two now to get ready to make their decisions. Give them time to pause, to remember, and to imagine.

3. Discuss the first question: What are the options?

Write this first question on the board under the decision point. If necessary, explain that *options* is a synonym for *choices*. Then invite students to brainstorm their ideas. You can do this by saying something like, "There are two obvious options: Yes, children under 14 SHOULD be allowed to work, or no, they should NOT be allowed to work."

Begin a numbered list of options on the board or chart. Record the two obvious ones you have just mentioned. Then point out that too often people consider only the most obvious options when there are others that are better.

Ask, "Can anyone think of other options besides these two?" (Possible answers: *The law could say that children under 14 could work just on weekends; children could only work if their grades were good; children could only do jobs that aren't dangerous and won't make them sick; children could work only where their parents work so someone would be there to watch out for them.*)

Add additional suggestions to the numbered list of options. Use prompt questions if needed to stimulate thinking. Thank students for their efforts and encourage everyone to participate. Remind them that the point of brainstorming is to think of as MANY things as possible and that there are no right or wrong, or good or bad answers.

4. Explain what "yardsticks" are and how they work.

Call attention to the yardsticks column on the poster. Tell students that although they probably have never thought of it before, thinking can be done well or it can be done poorly. By trying to think harder, anyone can usually think better—especially if the person thinks in certain ways. Explain that the yardsticks listed on the poster are reminders or suggestions for what to think about.

Point out that you have mentioned two obvious options and that students have come up with some good additional options. Ask everyone now to take a few minutes to think about some creative options—ones that haven't been thought of yet or ones that are new or unusual. (Possible answers: *Try to get rid of the law so children could work if they wanted to; try to change the law so children under 14 could work a little bit; try to convince adults that children can do work and earn their own money; schools could have a school-work program to train children to do things that adults do and get paid for it.*)

5. Discuss the second question: What are the reasons?

Have students review the list of options on the board and select two that they think have the most merit or promise. Mark these options on the board with a star or a check, or underline them.

Ask a volunteer to read the second question on the poster. Make sure that everyone understands that "pros" are reasons or arguments that support or are IN FAVOR OF something, and "cons" are reasons or arguments that oppose or are AGAINST something. Invite students to offer COMPLETE reasons—both pros and cons—for one of the starred options and record their suggestions on the board. (See page 52 for an example of how the lists on your chalkboard might develop.)

When students begin to run out of ideas, prompt them to use the yardsticks to help them think about whether they have thought of reasons for and against, different kinds of reasons, and hidden reasons. Encourage them to stretch their thinking and add more reasons to their list.

If necessary, explain that "different kinds of reasons" are reminders to make connections with all sorts of things related to the option, such as what the reasons would mean to their friends and their parents, to the economy; what effect their reasons would have on other workers; what the results would be in years ahead, and so on. You may also need to explain that "hidden reasons" are reminders to stretch their thinking and discover reasons that aren't thought of right away—ones that aren't obvious.

In the same manner, encourage responses for the second promising option on the list. Your classroom discussion of the first option might sound something like this:

Teacher: Let's talk about the school-work program first. Can anyone think of a reason that supports this option?

Student: Well, what if we want to work! If we made our own money, our parents wouldn't need to give us allowances. That would save them money.

Student: Another pro is that if work was a part of the school day, then teachers would make sure that the jobs were safe for us.

Student: The law could say that we could only work a certain number of hours a week and only do safe jobs.

Teacher: Good. Now think about some cons, or reasons against this option. Remember that the yardsticks include cons as well as pros so that you will think through each promising option as COMPLETELY as possible.

Student: Well, one con could be that we might not have enough time for classes or for our homework if we work.

Student: Another con is that some kids might not want to work and they shouldn't be forced into it.

Student: Yeah, and some of us have chores and things to do at home so we already work. And some kids do music and sports and other things after school.

Student: Also, some children could be given too much work to do or jobs that are too hard for them. Then they wouldn't do well in their school work.

Teacher: Okay, those are some good points. You've suggested several reasons as well as different kinds of reasons. Now try to think of some hidden reasons—reasons that you might not think of right away.

Student: I think one hidden reason has to do with how many jobs are available. If there aren't many jobs, we could be taking jobs away from adults and those who need the work more than we do.

Student: Another hidden reason against a student-work program is that it might be expensive for the schools to hire special teachers and buy materials for us to use.

Teacher: Yes, that's a possibility. These are all things that you will have to consider when you make your final choice about child labor.

6. Discuss the third question: What is the best choice?

Direct attention to the third powerful question and the yardsticks listed on the poster. Remind everyone that they are still thinking through, or weighing, the options.

Ask students to weigh all factors to make a realistic and careful choice. By considering the pros and cons of the most promising options, they should decide which option is best supported by important pros and least undermined by important cons. Have students consider the reasons that they gave for the first promising option. After students have had time to read and consider the listed reasons, ask for responses. Put stars or checks in front of the reasons that students select as most significant.

Students may now realize that all or most of the cons outweigh the pros for a school-work program. If this happens, you might ask if anyone wants to argue in favor of it. If students still think that the school-work program is NOT the best option, help them conclude that, by weighing all the factors, they have changed their opinions.

As a final note, you might explain that the original child welfare and labor law was written to protect children living at that time. People then were concerned that many children worked long hours at dangerous jobs, were underpaid, and could not attend school, thus prohibiting them from getting an education and better jobs.

Lead students in a discussion of the pros and cons of their other promising option. Remind everyone that the best careful choice is the option that has the most going for it and the least against it. Then ask them for their choice. Write it on the board as the best careful choice.

Because the steps in the Mental Management Strategy always enhance a lesson, you may wish to include Make Connections, Think About Thinking, or both of these post-task steps to round out the lesson.

7. Review the Decision-Making Strategy.

End the lesson by complimenting students on their work. Then use the poster and the students' responses to summarize the main steps in this strategy. Point out that they made a better decision than they would have if they had just stopped with the two obvious options. Remind them that they can even change their decision near the end of this process if there are important reasons for doing so. Emphasize the importance of what students have just learned.

Sample Chalkboard for the Children and Jobs Lesson

Decision Point: Whether or not children under 14 years of age should be allowed to work for pay

What are the options?

1. Allow children to work.
2. Don't allow children to work.
3. Allow children under 14 to work only on weekends.
4. Allow children to work only if their grades are good.
5. Allow children to work only where their parents work.
6. Allow work only if the job isn't dangerous or unhealthy.
7. Get rid of the law and let children work if and when they want.
8. Make new laws that require children to work a little.
☆ 9. <u>Make work a part of the school curriculum.</u>
☆ 10. <u>Allow children to work only after school a certain number of hours a week and only at safe jobs.</u>

What are the complete reasons for option #9?

Pros (reasons for)

* 1. If children earned money, parents would save money.
  2. Schools would make sure that children had safe jobs.

Cons (reasons against)

* 1. There wouldn't be enough time for classes or homework.
* 2. Some children already work at home so they wouldn't want to be forced to work at school.
  3. Some children do other things after school.
* 4. Children could be given so much hard work that they wouldn't do well in school.
* 5. Children might take work away from adults who really need to work.
* 6. It might be an expensive program for schools to run.

What are the complete reasons for option #10?

Pros (reasons for)

* 1. It gives parents and children a choice about working.
* 2. It allows children to work a little each week.
* 3. It won't cost the school anything.
* 4. Children will make their own money.
* 5. Children will be safe.

Cons (reasons against)

  1. Children may want to work but their parents won't let them.
* 2. Children might take jobs away from adults.
  3. Children may not be able to find jobs.

What is the best careful choice?

Allow children to work only after school a certain number of hours a week, and only at safe jobs.

Classroom Guide

1. Direct attention to the poster.

Ask students to name times when they or adults have had to make decisions. Have students speculate about what often happens when people don't properly think through the decisions that they make.

2. Present the decision point for students to consider.

On the board, write the decision point that students will consider. Then suggest that they take a minute or two to Get Ready for the task. (If necessary, remind them to pause, to remember, and to imagine.)

3. Discuss the first question: What are the options?

After students have had time to think, record the options that they suggest on the board. Use prompt questions if necessary to help them brainstorm.

4. Explain what "yardsticks" are and how they work.

Call students' attention to the yardsticks listed on the poster and, without matching each of their responses to a certain yardstick, ask students to consider whether or not they have measured up to all of the yardsticks. Add more options to the list as students suggest them.

5. Discuss the second question: What are the reasons?

Have students review the options on their list and choose the two most promising ones. Mark each of these with a star. Then have students consider reasons, both pros and cons, for each of the two promising options. Give prompts only as necessary and use the yardsticks to check progress.

6. Discuss the third question: What is the best choice?

Use the yardsticks to help students carefully weigh the pro and con reasons. Mark each of the most important pros and cons with a star. Ask students to make their best careful decision—the realistic choice with the most important pros that outweigh the negative reasons. Record their choice. Remember that students need not all make the same choice, but they should be able to support their choice with reasons.

7. Review the Decision-Making Strategy.

Conclude by complimenting students and summarizing the main steps of this strategy. Emphasize the importance of this process and the effect of it on their thinking.

After-the-Lesson Checklist

- Did you explain why decision-making skills are important?

- Did you convey to students the main points of this strategy without belaboring the lesson?

- Did you use ideas from the sample lesson as necessary?

- Did you encourage students to use the yardsticks?

Teachers' Questions and Authors' Answers

Q: I already use some thinking skills in the classroom. Why should I teach this strategy?

A: It's great that you already use some thinking skills in the classroom, but we would like to point out some subtleties in this strategy that are very important as they may help your students do an even better job of thinking. While many teachers lead brainstorming activities, for example, the use of the yardsticks is not common. Using this tactic will systematically teach students how to do progressive thinking, step-by-step, and expand their options.

Also, the three powerful questions used in this strategy provide students with a direct way to organize and focus their thinking. Teachers who have used this strategy have found that the approach with its three questions makes it easier to infuse into subject matter contexts.

Finally, this and other strategies in this program foster metacognition (thinking about thinking), which research has shown is crucial to good thinking.

Q: I can't seem to think of any places to introduce decision points. What do you suggest?

A: Thinking of your curriculum in terms of good decision points may be new to you. The first thing to do is get out the textbooks and other materials that you use along with your lesson plans. Look for places in the upcoming weeks' lessons where someone has already made a choice or is about to make a choice (fact or fiction). Perhaps students themselves will need to make a choice that pertains to the lesson. As you can see, many opportunities for places to infuse can begin to open up to you.

Think also of the daily events in the lives of your students—in their relationships, in their activities, in their learning—in AND out of school. This will also suggest decision points. Another source of suggestions for decision points can be found in the Teacher Resources section at the end of this module under "Opportunities in Your Daily Curriculum."

Finally, as you go through the first weeks of practice with the strategy, other teachers (and even your students) may suggest decision points that will surprise you—and make you think of many more!

WHAT ARE THE OPTIONS? *Concentrated Practices*

Purpose of these Practices

This practice stresses the importance of thinking deliberately and carefully, rather than hastily, about the choices available when faced with a decision. By learning to consider many options, students will get over their tendency to approach problems as simple either-or choices. Instead, they will learn to brainstorm numerous and creative choices.

There is another advantage to exploring options. By thinking through possible alternatives as decision points in the curriculum, students will gain a deeper understanding of the subject matter that they are studying.

Preparation

- Display the Decision-Making poster in a prominent place in the classroom.

- Read through the Classroom Guide on the next page.

- Identify four subject areas, topics and decision points for the remaining four days of the week in which students can practice this step. Formulate decision points that will easily generate a list of options. Record these in the Weekly Planner on page 79. Some possibilities are:

History	Did the colonists have other options besides "throwing" the Boston Tea Party?
Reading	What options did a particular character in a story have?
Mathematics	What are your options when faced with a problem about measurements that you don't understand?
Health	What are the options that young people have when someone encourages them to try drugs?
Spelling	What are the options for remembering a spelling rule, such as when to double the final consonant before a suffix is added?

(See page 84 for additional suggestions.)

- Use the Working Outline on page 80 to make notes, recommendations, or changes in your daily lesson plans.

Approximate Classroom Time Needed

WEEK 5   Tuesday – Friday: *20 minutes each day*

Classroom Guide

1. Call attention to the poster.

Tell students that although they did very well in going through all the steps in the Decision-Making Strategy, they will become even better thinkers after they have more experience practicing each step individually. Point out the first question: What are the options? Explain that for the next four days they will concentrate on how to answer this powerful question.

2. Present the decision point for students to consider.

On the board or chart paper, write the decision point that you have prepared for this practice. You may want to allow a few moments for students to get ready for this task by pausing, remembering, and imagining.

3. Ask students for options.

Encourage everyone to brainstorm a list of options. Record all suggestions without commenting on their worth.

4. Ask students to use the yardsticks to measure their list of options.

Use the yardsticks to prompt thinking about more options and creative ones. Add the new suggestions to the list. After a number of options have been suggested, you may wish to have students look over the list once again to see if they have measured up to all of the yardsticks.

5. Conclude the practice.

Compliment students on their work. Make the point that students have made progress in their ability to make decisions. Point out that they went beyond the obvious options to list many others, including some new and creative ones. Reinforce the point that obvious options are not always the best ones and that they can come up with better solutions at decision points when they try harder.

Note: Preserve the lists of options that students generate during the practices this week. These lists can be used in later practice sessions for this strategy. If you prefer using the chalkboard rather than chart paper to record responses during the lessons, you might have volunteers copy the lists onto chart paper at the end of each practice session.

A Classroom Example

You have decided to highlight a science lesson on the environment and have chosen a problem from your local community for students to consider—a polluted river. Your practice session might develop something like the following. (See page 69 for an example of how the list of options might develop.)

Teacher: You all know that no one is allowed to swim in the river anymore because it is so polluted that the water could make you sick. The decision to forbid swimming was made by our local government to protect the people who live here.

The teacher writes the following decision point on the chalkboard: Should local authorities have forbidden swimming in the polluted river?

Teacher: I'd like you now to focus on the first powerful question of the Decision-Making Strategy and think about what OTHER options might be considered. Any ideas?

Student: Well, they could have made the other obvious decision and NOT have forbidden swimming.

Student: Yeah, they could have put up a sign saying it might be dangerous and let people decide for themselves if they want to swim in the river.

Student: They could tell us WHERE it's okay to swim.

Teacher: Good suggestions. I think I've listed all of them. But what about the yardsticks? Have we come up with any creative options or different kinds of options yet?

Student: No, not really I was thinking that the mayor could decide to clean the river up rather than closing it.

Student: Yeah! And everyone who uses the river could help.

Student: But the pollution might be chemicals and stuff that you can't just pick up. They should find out who's doing the polluting and make THEM clean it up and stop polluting.

Teacher: So have we been creative and varied enough with our ideas? If so, we can move on.

Student: No, our ideas are really the usual ones that everyone always thinks of. Maybe they could allow swimming, but only in scuba gear!

Student: Or close the river to people who fish and go boating, too, so more people would work harder to get the river cleaned up faster.

The teacher announces that they only have time for three more options, then concludes the session.

After-the-Lesson Checklist

- Did you give students enough time to think?
- Did you encourage using the yardsticks but refrain from matching each response to a corresponding yardstick?
- Did you wrap up the practice within about 20 minutes?
- Did you integrate the practice into your usual curriculum?

Teachers' Questions and Authors' Answers

Q: I get confused about the yardsticks and how to use them. What do you suggest?

A: The yardsticks are intended to serve as guides to aid and extend thinking. They will help students determine whether their thinking about one of the questions was thorough. When you notice that students are ignoring an important yardstick, ask for an answer that will fulfill it. For example, "Aren't there any additional options besides these obvious ones?" You could also prompt students with specific questions about the options already mentioned.

It isn't important to label each answer as "obvious," "many," or "creative" as often these categories overlap. The important thing is that students have a sense that some of the ideas they had were obvious, some were additional, and some were creative.

Q: I believe that using this strategy is worthwhile, but I just don't know where I'm going to find the time to do it.

A: Time is often mentioned as a problem for teachers when something new is introduced into the curriculum. Remember, however, that this is not something you should simply add on as a separate part of the school day. Rather, find places in your lessons where you can have students use a strategy, or a part of a strategy, to give them a chance to gain deeper understanding of whatever it is they are already studying. Think of this not as more or additional work, but rather as a better way or method to reinforce learning.

You might also benefit from some of the time-saving tips that have been mentioned before: set limits to the number of responses or answers you will accept; if you have a talkative group, call on each student once during a practice rather than during every discussion; have students work on paper or in groups—especially if they are already engaged in writing or group work. Remember, too, that the more you work with these strategies, the more efficient you will become.

Purpose of these Practices

Searching for COMPLETE reasons teaches students to avoid several common pitfalls when making decisions: thinking only about reasons for one or two favorite options, thinking only of the pro (in favor of) reasons, and limiting the number of reasons to only one or two for each option.

During this step in the Decision-Making Strategy, students learn to think of many reasons, different kinds of reasons, and hidden reasons for their options. By using this second powerful question and the yardsticks, students learn to thoughtfully and thoroughly evaluate their options before carefully making a final choice.

Preparation

■ Display the Decision-Making poster in a prominent place in the classroom.

■ Read through the Classroom Guide on the next page.

■ For each day this week, have ready the decision points along with the lists of options generated by students last week. Record the decision points in your Weekly Planner on page 79 along with the subject and topic you plan to use. If you prefer, you could generate new decision points for the practices this week. If you do this, have students quickly develop a list of options when the lesson begins or, to save time, have a list of options already prepared.

■ When you decide to have students work in discussion groups, you may wish to have copies of the list of options available for their use.

■ Use the Working Outline on page 81 to make notes, recommendations, or changes in your daily lesson plans.

Approximate Classroom Time Needed

WEEK 6   Monday: *40 minutes*
Tuesday – Friday: *20 minutes each day*

Classroom Guide

1. Present the decision point and the options to be considered today.

Have this information displayed for all to see. Quickly help students review today's decision point and the options that accompany them.

2. Direct attention to the poster.

Point out the second question: What are the complete reasons for the most promising options? Remind students that they previously practiced this step when they were introduced to the Decision-Making Strategy. Explain that each day this week, they will consider a different decision point with options. Doing this will help them learn to really give a lot of thought to reasons—both pro and con—and become better thinkers.

3. Have students discuss the complete reasons, pros and cons, by using the yardsticks.

This step can be done with the entire class as was done in the Orientation Lesson. However, this would be an ideal time for students to work in discussion groups so that they can more quickly share their thoughts, arrive at well thought out reasons, and perhaps form a consensus. If you feel that your students are ready for it today, guide them in forming manageable groups. Suggest that someone in each group record the reasons for the two or three most promising options.

As students are doing this, walk around and give encouragement and support. Ask guiding questions, such as: Can you think of any cons, or reasons against—not just reasons for—that option? Did you use the yardsticks before you considered the next option?

After about ten minutes, ask the groups to review the work they have done so that each recorder can finalize the group's complete reasons, pro and con.

4. Invite each group to share some element of their discussion.

To maximize participation and touch briefly on the major points that have been covered, ask a spokesperson from each group to share only a highlight from the group's discussion. You can do this by asking questions such as:

- Which options did your group choose as the most promising?

- What did your group think of as the pro reasons for one of your most promising options?

- Did any group have any cons for the same option?

- Who else came up with other reasons, either pro or con, for the same option?

■ When you considered the yardsticks, were you able to think of hidden reasons?

5. Conclude the practice.

Compliment students on their thoughtful work, both in their groups and when they shared their thoughts with the class. Remind them that selecting the most promising options and considering reasons both for and against each option will definitely help them make better decisions. Point out that they will also have a better understanding of why some decisions that they, or others, have made resulted in a choice they were happy with or in one they later regretted.

Note: Record the two or three most promising options with the complete reasons, both pro and con, for use next week when students practice making a choice.

A Classroom Example

You have decided to continue with the problem of the polluted river for today. You have saved the list of options for this decision point from last week and have posted it on the board for all to see. You have also decided to have students work in small groups today. Your practice session might develop something like the following. (See page 69 for an example of how the lists of pros and cons for these options might develop.)

Teacher: Today we're going to continue to explore the polluted river decision point and the list of options that I saved from your work last week. Take a moment now to Get Ready and then we'll begin.

After a moment, the teacher asks students to form small groups. When the groups are settled, the teacher suggests that someone in each group serve as recorder and make a list of the pros and cons for each option.

Teacher: I would like you all to take about ten minutes to think and talk about the options listed here. Each group should choose two or three of the most promising options and then list COMPLETE reasons for each one. Remember to use the yardsticks to guide your thinking. Afterwards, you will have a chance to share some of your group's ideas with the rest of the class.

After giving a few reminders about the rules of small group discussion, the teacher walks around the room, stopping at each group to offer encouragement or prompts.

Teacher: You have a lot of pros for that option. Can you think of any cons?

Teacher: How are the reasons measuring up to the yardsticks?

Teacher: Have you thought about WHO will do that or HOW that will be done?

The teacher gives a warning that two minutes remain for groups to wrap up their discussions, then invites volunteers from each group to share parts of their work.

Teacher: Shari, what options did your group star as most promising?

Shari: We starred two of them: number 4—having the people who use the river clean it up, and number 5—having the companies that do the polluting clean it up.

Teacher: Thank you. Who else chose option 4 or option 5? Okay, David, can you give us the pros for option 4?

After David gives his group's list of pros, the teacher asks for a list of cons from another group that has chosen this option. The teacher continues in this manner with the other promising option, and if time permits, a third option could also be explored.

After-the-Lesson Checklist

- Did you use and reinforce the wording shown on the poster?

- Did you explain that not all of their responses will be acknowledged because of time limitations?

- Did most students participate in group brainstorming?

- Did you remind students to use the yardsticks?

- Did you end the lesson with a summary and a comment about the importance of the lesson?

Teachers' Questions and Authors' Answers

Q: I like to ask questions that challenge my students to think, but I never know what to expect. How can I cope with crazy answers?

A: When students are given an opportunity to offer creative ideas, teachers may be caught off guard with some responses. As you and your students continue to practice the strategies, the novelty will wear off and everyone will concentrate on the end results—better thinking. In the meantime, here are a few suggestions:

- Don't overreact. Treat all ideas equally and record them on the board or chart. Don't give hints about which ideas you think are worthwhile OR crazy. Students may test you and if you don't react to silly or distasteful responses, eventually they will disappear.

- Make a disclaimer. Make it clear before you begin a session that you do not necessarily agree or disagree with what you write on the board. Rather, you are recording THEIR ideas. You do not take responsibility for their ideas; the students must take that responsibility.

- Be open-minded. Some of the "crazy" ideas that students come up with may lead to something worthwhile, or they may be the product of a very creative mind, or reflect the thinking of a student who thinks quite differently from you or everyone else. It may take a while to understand this way of thinking. During the group sessions, students have an opportunity to explore each others' ideas and come to a consensus. At that time, some of the "crazy" ideas may be refined into very usable and effective ones.

Q: Won't it be frustrating to students to go through the decision-making process and then not be able to actually follow through on the decision?

A: Yes, this is possible and we encourage teachers to find places in the curriculum where students CAN follow through. For example, while studying hazards to the environment, students made and followed up on decisions about cleaning up their local environment by starting recycling programs; during a lesson on health and safety, students made a decision to make their neighborhood safer by enlisting parents and neighbors in crime watch programs.

On the other hand, it is worth mentioning that students are NOT turned off by decision points when they know that they have little or no influence over them. During these first weeks and months of practice with this and the other strategies, it is important for you to select varied spots throughout the curriculum that will promote worthwhile thinking and be of interest to students.

Purpose of these Practices

This practice will teach students how to arrive at conclusions by weighing all factors to make a careful choice. Students have already considered and limited their options to the two or three most promising ones. Now they will weigh the pros and cons of these options against each other to decide which option is most solid. They learn that although there may be reasons against their best choice, the reasons FOR it outweigh them.

This final step stresses the necessity to support decisions with important reasons. It teaches students to make thoughtful decisions rather than hasty ones. Each of these practices will also enhance the material that you present by giving students opportunities for thoughtful analysis, discussion, and decision-making.

Preparation

■ Display the Decision-Making poster in a prominent place in the classroom.

■ Read through the Classroom Guide on the next page.

■ Decide which three days this week you will use this practice session. Either select three decision points along with their options and reasons from the previous practice, or prepare new decision points with options and reasons. Record this information in the Weekly Planner on page 79. Some possible new decision points are:

Social Studies	Whether or not you would migrate to the United States if you lived in Ireland during the Great Potato Famine.
Reading	If you were the boy in the story *Old Yeller*, what would you have done about your dog?
Health	If you thought that a friend had lied to you, what would you do?

(See page 84 for additional suggestions.)

■ Use the Working Outline on page 82 to make notes recommendations, or changes in your daily lesson plans.

Approximate Classroom Time Needed

WEEK 7   Any three days: *20 minutes each day*

Classroom Guide

1. Present the decision point and the options to be considered today.

Have this information displayed for all to see. You might suggest that students take a few minutes to Get Ready. If you are using material from a previous session, ask students to review the decision point, the most promising options that they selected, and the complete reasons (both pro and con). If you prepared a new decision point, ask the class to quickly decide on two or three most promising options with complete reasons.

2. Direct attention to the poster.

Point out the third question (What is the best choice?) and its yardsticks. Ask students to consider all of the reasons listed and to decide which ones are the most important. Explain that doing this will help them choose the option that is the best choice—the most realistic and thoughtful one. Remind everyone that the important reasons can either be for or against an option. Then give them time to think.

3. Have students choose the most important reasons.

Invite students to give their opinions and mark each reason mentioned with a star. During this process, remember to refrain from making judgments or showing preference for some choices over others.

4. Have students decide on the best option.

Remind them to consider which option is best supported by important pros and least damaging cons. Warn students that they must be able to support their final choice with reasons that are important to them. Reassure everyone that there is really no "right" answer and that all of them may not make the same decision. Then have students make a final choice.

5. Conclude the lesson.

If time permits, have students do the Make Connections and/or Think About Thinking steps. Then compliment students on their thoughtful work and summarize how they arrived at their best careful choices. Point out how the Decision-Making Strategy helped them reach a decision that was both thoughtful and intelligent.

A Classroom Example

You have decided to continue with the problem of the polluted river for today. You have saved the lists of options and complete reasons for this decision point and have posted them for all to see. (See the Sample

Chalkboard for this problem on page 69.) Your practice session might develop something like this:

Teacher: Let's consider the final step of the Decision-Making Strategy today for the polluted river decision. We will start by reviewing the promising options and the complete reasons that the class came up with last week. Then we will make our best, careful choice about the options. Look at Step 3 on the poster. What does it tell us to do?

Student: To weigh all factors. What does that mean?

Teacher: It means to think everything through carefully and make decisions about which reasons are the most realistic and important ones. So look them over and tell me which reasons are most important. I'll mark them with a star.

Student: I think it's really important to get the river cleaned up. That's a pro under both options.

Student: Yes, and it's important that it ALL gets cleaned up, which means the poisons as well as the garbage. So put a star by the con reason under option 4.

Student: And it's also a star for the pro under option 5. It would take experts to know how to remove the poisons from the water. Volunteers couldn't do that.

The teacher lets the discussion continue a few minutes longer then asks students to make a choice, to decide which option is supported by the strongest reasons—the one with the most starred pros and the least starred cons.

Student: Option 5 only has one con with a star.

Student: And it has stars by all of the pro reasons.

Student: All of the pros for option 4 really are included in option 5, too, so it's probably the best choice.

Teacher: Does it SEEM like it should be the best choice?

Student: Yes it does. Do you know if that's what the city is trying to do?

No one knows for sure and a suggestion is made to share the result of their thinking about this problem with the Mayor's office. All agree. The teacher congratulates students on their careful examination of this decision point and concludes the lesson.

After-the-Lesson Checklist

- Did you refrain from showing preference for some choices?

- Did students understand that they did not all have to agree?

- Did you bring out the fact that students should be able to support their final choices with important reasons?

- Did you use one or more of the Mental Management steps?

Teachers' Questions and Authors' Answers

Q: Although I like the material in this program, it's still difficult to find time for the sessions. Any suggestions?

A: We realize that this is a highly interactive process for you and your students. You are asking students to think and then express their ideas. Here are two ways to save time after the initial practice weeks:

- Give students copies of the worksheets provided at the end of this module in the Teacher Resources section and have them work in groups. Assign groups and give students time to figure out how to work together. This process may not seem like a time-saver to you, but with a little practice, cooperative learning DOES save time and helps students learn to think. It also creates synergism. Students feed on each others' ideas and come up with new and creative ones. Your role during the group sessions is to monitor the groups and give guidance ONLY when necessary. If students are doing well, just move on. Try it!

- Students can also do independent work, either in school or at home. Once again, provide them with the worksheets. From time to time, ask if any students wish to share with the class any decision points that they have considered and thought through. This will not only give recognition to students for their successful efforts, but may offer other students ideas for solutions to similar situations.

Q: My students definitely seem to understand the strategy. How do I actually know if they are learning to think better?

A: This is really not a "testing" issue. Thinking skills are not something that you or your students should approach as one more thing for them to cram into their heads for a test. Rather, it's a developed talent that they need to practice and internalize over a period of time. There are no quick-and-easy ways or any tests to determine if your students are learning the strategies and thinking better.

What you CAN do is observe students and listen for evidence that they are using the strategies. One sure and positive sign is hearing students suggest using a strategy when you haven't even thought of it! Also, listen for the use of thinking vocabulary and buzz words during the day.

A second way to determine their success and progress is to ask students to use the strategies, on their own or in groups, without evaluation from you. This gives them the chance to develop a certain autonomy in their thinking. This is important if students are to become able to put thinking skills to work both inside and outside the classroom.

Sample Chalkboard for the Polluted River Problem

Decision Point: Should the local authorities have forbidden swimming in the polluted river?

What are the options?

1. Not forbid swimming.

2. Put up a sign saying the water might be dangerous and let people decide whether or not to swim.

3. Tell people where they can and cannot swim in the river.

☆ 4. <u>Ask for clean-up help from people who use the river.</u>

☆ 5. <u>Ask the mayor to find out which companies are doing the polluting. Make them stop it and do the cleanup.</u>

6. Allow swimming only for people who wear scuba gear.

7. Forbid fishing and boating, too, so more people would work harder to clear up the river.

What are the complete reasons for option # 4?

Pros (reasons for)

* 1. The river will get clean.

* 2. It will save money. People would be volunteers.

3. The clean up would get people together, and they would meet each other and become friends.

Cons (reasons against)

* 1. People might not volunteer.

* 2. Even if people did volunteer, the river might not get cleaned because there are some things that can't just be picked up.

* 3. If the river is too polluted, it could make people sick just trying to clean out the garbage and junk.

What are the complete reasons for option #5?

Pros (reasons for)

* 1. The river would get clean.

* 2. The companies would pay to clean up their own mess.

* 3. The companies could hire pollution specialists to make recommendations.

* 4. They could call in experts to clean up industrial waste before it is discharged into the river.

* 5. They would be more careful in the future so they wouldn't have to go through all the clean up again.

Cons (reasons against)

1. Companies might claim that they weren't responsible.

* 2. They might delay doing anything.

3. They might do just a little something to the water to make it look better but that wouldn't really get out all the pollution.

What is the best careful choice?

Ask the mayor to find out which companies are doing the polluting in order to make them stop it and clean it up.

Purpose of these Practices

As the proverb says, "Practice makes perfect." By asking students to apply the whole strategy to decision points, the lessons this week will pull together everything that they have learned in the past three weeks. Using all of the skills they have learned will enable them to become good critical thinkers as well as decision makers.

These initial weeks of practice will reward you, too. You will gain confidence in conducting the sessions, using the strategies or selected parts of a strategy, and identifying situations that seem to invite thoughtful reflection by your students. In this way, you can add interest and depth of understanding to the various subjects that you teach.

Preparation

■ Display the Decision-Making poster in a prominent place in the classroom.

■ Read through the Classroom Guide on the next page.

■ Decide which three days this week you will use this practice session. Select three new decision points to use with the complete strategy. Or you could ask students if they have any pressing decisions to make at school, at home, or in any other part of their lives. Record the decision points in your Weekly Planner on page 79. Some possible subject areas and topics are:

Social Studies	President Lincoln's decision to declare war on the South
Reading	Huckleberry Finn's decision about turning Jim in as a runaway slave
Language	Should elementary school students be required to learn a second language?
General	What should be done about messy desks in the classroom?

(See page 84 for additional suggestions.)

■ Think through how each lesson might unfold as you guide students through the steps of this strategy. Use the Working Outline on page 83 for notes about modeling, prompt questions, or reminders that you might use.

■ Have copies of the Decision-Making Checklist on page 78 to give to students.

Approximate Classroom Time Needed

WEEK 8   Any three days: *45 minutes each day*

Classroom Guide

1. Present the decision point for students to consider.

Begin by asking students to take some time to Get Ready for today's task. If necessary, remind them how to prepare themselves by pausing, remembering, and imagining. Give them a minute or so to do this as you write the decision point for today on the board or chart.

2. Distribute the checklists and have students consider the first question: What are the options?

Explain that today students will use worksheets and work quietly on their own at first. Tell them that they won't have to turn in their papers unless they want to discuss their work with you later. Give the class about five minutes to consider the decision point and write at least four options on their worksheets.

3. Ask students to use the yardsticks to expand each other's list of options.

Have students exchange papers with a partner. Ask them to consider the options listed by their classmate and then think of at least four more. Indicate the poster and remind students to use the yardsticks. Encourage them to really stretch their thinking and branch out in different directions so that they include less obvious and creative options. After about five minutes, ask students to return the papers to their partners.

4. Have students consider the second question: What are the reasons?

Encourage students to carefully consider the expanded list of options. Ask them to put a star in front of the two or three most promising ones. Then give them about ten minutes to list COMPLETE reasons (both pros and cons) for each promising option. Remind them to use the yardsticks.

5. Invite students to answer the third question: What is the best choice?

Suggest that students carefully reflect on and weigh the reasons for each option and then make their decision. Remind them to be realistic and to be ready to support their final choice with the most important reasons. After about five minutes, allow those who wish to share their decisions and reasons with the class to do so.

6. Conclude the practice.

Suggest that everyone take a few minutes to do one or both of the Mental Management post-task steps. If necessary, offer prompts for the Make Connections step by asking: "How does the thinking task you just completed connect to other things you know about? What BIG ideas do you have?" For the Think About Thinking step, ask the questions: "What went well? What was hard? What improvements can you make?"

Compliment students on their efforts to master this strategy. Encourage them to continue using it and remind them that using this strategy will help them become better thinkers AND better decision-makers. If time permits, reinforce today's learning by summarizing the main points of this practice. (As this week progresses, give fewer and fewer prompts during the practice sessions in order that students can assume more responsibility for their learning.)

A Classroom Example

You have chosen to use a decision point about American history today: If you lived during the Civil War, which side would you have supported—the North or the South? Your practice session might develop something like this:

Teacher: We're going to put together all of the steps of the Decision-Making Strategy today. Use the poster if you need help remembering what to do. The decision point is one that concerns our nation between 1861 and 1864—the Civil War. Many Americans had to decide whether to fight for slavery and secession from the Union, or against them. What would you have done?

As the teacher writes the decision point on the board, he or she suggests that students take a moment to Get Ready.

Teacher: Today I'm going to ask you to start by doing some thinking by yourselves. Use these worksheets I'm passing out to record your ideas. If you need more space to write, just use the back of the worksheet. You won't have to turn this in unless you want me to review it. Now think about the first question and write down at least four options. Don't forget to use the yardsticks to help you.

After about five minutes, the teacher asks students to trade papers with a partner and add at least four more options to that person's list. Giving students another five minutes to work, the teacher begins to walk around the room, offering encouragement, prompts, and assistance if needed.

Teacher: Now return your lists to their original owners and carefully look through all of the options listed. Which ones do you think are the best or most promising ones? Choose two or three and mark them with a star. Then you know what to do! List the reasons for the options you have chosen. Take your time and remember to think of both pros and cons.

Again, the teacher circulates among the students for about ten minutes. Afterward, the teacher prompts students to go on to the final question and make their choice. After about five minutes, the teacher invites students to share their final decision.

Teacher: I would have been on the side of the North.

Teacher: Why? Give the reasons you have for your decision.

As students present their decisions and reasons, a debate begins. As necessary, the teacher reminds students to let each other speak, to listen to and respect the opinions of others, and to seriously consider the explanations being given. The teacher points out what a difficult decision this must have been for many people during the Civil War and then concludes the lesson.

After-the-Lesson Checklist

■ Did students know how to do the strategy with only a few prompts, if any, from you?

■ Did you refrain from showing preferences when students shared their ideas with the class?

■ Did you use all or part of the Mental Management Strategy?

■ Are you trying out various classroom arrangements, such as students working alone, with partners, and in groups?

Teachers' Questions and Authors' Answers

Q: Now that I have finished this last week of the Decision-Making Strategy, what should I do with it?

A: First of all, congratulations on your weeks of hard work! Now in order for your students to continue to benefit from and retain their new skills, it is important to keep this strategy alive in your classroom.

We suspect that you have become very adept at identifying decision points in your curriculum. If so, continue to pinpoint these places as you plan your lessons and use all or part of the this strategy. At other times, you and your students may find a place to infuse the strategy on the spur of the moment while a lesson is in progress. It needn't always take formal planning.

But if even selecting opportunities and infusing this strategy still seem to be somewhat of an effort for you, we hope that you will continue to follow our suggestions and teach the strategy until the process becomes second nature to you. As long as YOU find the process to be an effort, your students will probably be struggling with it, too. Keep in mind that good decision-making skills are vital to your students. These skills cannot be internalized without repeated and continuous practice. These initial weeks of practice that you and your students have put in will be wasted unless you keep the strategy alive in your classroom.

We suggest that you use all or part of the strategy at least once each week. Always follow through when students suggest a place in the curriculum where a decision point, one or more of the questions of this strategy, or the complete decision-making process would be useful. Have confidence, as we do, that you can help your students become better, more thoughtful decision-makers.

Contents and Notes

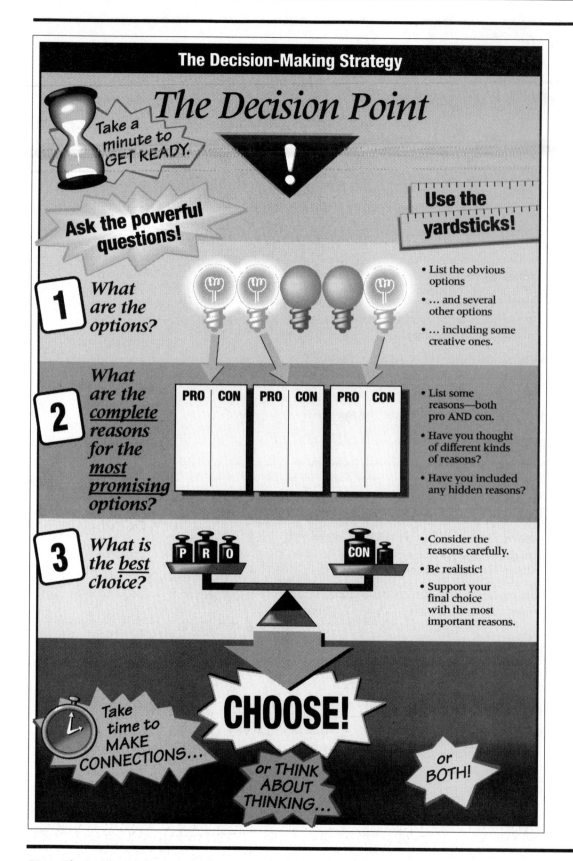

The Decision-Making Strategy

The Decision Point

Take a minute to GET READY.

Ask the powerful questions!

1 What are the options?

- List the obvious options
- ... and several other options
- ... including some creative ones.

2 What are the *complete* reasons for the *most promising* options?

PRO	CON	PRO	CON	PRO	CON

- List some reasons—both pro AND con.
- Have you thought of different kinds of reasons?
- Have you included any hidden reasons?

3 What is the *best* choice?

PRO   CON

- Consider the reasons carefully.
- Be realistic!
- Support your final choice with the most important reasons.

Use the yardsticks!

Take time to MAKE CONNECTIONS...

CHOOSE!

or THINK ABOUT THINKING...

or BOTH!

The Decision-Making Strategy Worksheet

Decision Point:

Get Ready: Pause...Remember...Imagine...

1. What are the options?

_____   _____

_____   _____

_____   _____

2. What are the complete reasons for one promising option?

Pros   *Cons*

_____   _____

_____   _____

_____   _____

_____   _____

What are the complete reasons for another promising option?

Pros   *Cons*

_____   _____

_____   _____

_____   _____

_____   _____

3. What is the best careful choice? Give reasons for your choice.

_____

_____

_____

Make Connections

What does this remind you of? _____

Think About Thinking

What went well? _____

What was hard? _____

What can be improved? _____

The Decision-Making Checklist

Make sure to...
- record ALL ideas.
- do every step.
- always use the yardsticks.

If you are working in a group, make sure that...
- everyone participates.
- there is NO criticism of the ideas of others.

Decision Point:

Get Ready

❏ *Pause.*   ❏ *Remember.*   ❏ *Imagine.*

1. Options

List all the options you can think of. Use these yardsticks to help you.
- ❏ obvious options
- ❏ several more options
- ❏ new, creative options

2. Complete Reasons

List all the reasons you can think of for two or three of the most promising options. Use these yardsticks to help you.
- ❏ some reasons, both pro and con
- ❏ different kinds of reasons, pro and con
- ❏ hidden reasons, pro and con

3. Best Careful Choice

- ❏ Which option is supported by the most important reasons?
- ❏ Remember to be realistic!
- ❏ Be prepared to support your choice with reasons.

❏ *Make Connections*   ❏ *Think About Thinking*

WEEK 5: ORIENTATION LESSON & WHAT ARE THE OPTIONS? PRACTICES

MONDAY	TUESDAY	WEDNESDAY	THURSDAY	FRIDAY
Orientation Social Studies: Children & Jobs Should children under 14 be allowed to work?	*Options Practice* Subject & Topic Decision Point:	*Options Practice* Subject & Topic Decision Point:	*Options Practice* Subject & Topic Decision Point:	*Options Practice* Subject & Topic Decision Point:

WEEK 6: WHAT ARE THE REASONS? PRACTICES

MONDAY	TUESDAY	WEDNESDAY	THURSDAY	FRIDAY
Subject & Topic Decision Point:	Subject & Topic Decision Point:	Subject & Topic Decision Point:	Subject & Topic Decision Point:	Subject & Topic Decision Point:

WEEK 7: WHAT IS THE BEST CHOICE? PRACTICES

MONDAY	TUESDAY	WEDNESDAY	THURSDAY	FRIDAY
Subject & Topic Decision Point:		Subject & Topic Decision Point:		Subject & Topic Decision Point:

WEEK 8: PULLING IT ALL TOGETHER

MONDAY	TUESDAY	WEDNESDAY	THURSDAY	FRIDAY
Subject & Topic Decision Point:		Subject & Topic Decision Point:		Subject & Topic Decision Point:

Working Outline: **What Are the Options?**

1. Present the decision point for students to consider.

2. Call attention to the poster and the first powerful question: What are the options?

3. Ask students to brainstorm a list of options and record all responses.

4. Ask students to use the yardsticks to measure their list of options and add less obvious, more creative ones.

5. Conclude with praise and a brief review or summary. Decide if you will save the lists for later use.

Working Outline: **What Are the Reasons?**

1. Present the decision point and the options to be considered today.

2. Direct attention to the second question on the poster: What are the COMPLETE reasons?

3. Have students work in groups and use the yardsticks to form a list of reasons, both pro and con, for the most promising options.

4. Have a spokesperson from each group share a highlight of the discussion. Use prompt questions to keep them focused.

5. Conclude with praise and a reminder of the importance of what they are doing. Decide if you will save two or three of the most promising options for later use.

1. Present the decision point and the options to be considered today.

2. Focus attention on the third question on the poster: What is the best careful choice? Have them use the yardsticks to consider the reasons.

3. Have students choose the most important reasons, both pro and con. Mark each with a star.

4. Ask students to make their best careful choice.

5. Conclude with praise and a brief review or summary.

Working Outline: **Pulling It All Together**

1. Present the decision point for students to consider. Give them time to Get Ready.

2. Have students consider the first question: What are the options? Distribute the Checklists and have them work alone to list four options.

3. Ask students to exchange papers with a partner and use the yardsticks to add four more options.

4. Have students consider the second question: What are the reasons? On their own papers, have them mark the most promising options, then list COMPLETE reasons for each.

5. Ask students to review the reasons and answer the final question: What is the best choice?

6. Conclude with one or both of the post-task steps, Make Connections and Think About Thinking. Compliment students and stress the importance of thoughtful decision-making.

Opportunities in Your Daily Curriculum

The Decision-Making Strategy can be applied in many places throughout your curriculum and daily classroom life. Develop and present decision points as questions. For example:

- Should animals be dissected in class?

- What should be done about the use of toxic pesticides?

- In the story, Jack and the Beanstalk, should Jack have traded his cow for the magic beans?

- Should the United States adopt the metric system?

- If you were the Vice President of the United States, would you run for the presidency?

The list below offers some suggestions for places where you might develop decision points and infuse an isolated question (What are the options? What are the reasons? What is the best choice?) or the entire strategy. You will find that you have many more ideas that are specific to your classes. Expand and adapt this list for future use. Be sure to share and exchange your ideas with other teachers.

Science
dissection of animals in class
use of toxic pesticides
building of a proposed dam
fluoride in drinking water
logging of old-growth forests

Social Studies
the funding of Captain Cook's
   expedition to the North Pole
USA's quota of refugee immigrants
terrorism
prisoners of war
Lincoln's assassination
selection of the president
peaceful demonstrations

Language Arts
Jack and the Beanstalk
tall tales
doing research for a report
use of slang
reading nonfiction
making an outline
grammar rules

Music
learning to play an instrument
a marching band
classical music
hard rock music
concerts

Art
touching objects in art galleries
projects for next week
drawing likenesses of people
rules in the art room

Health
required vaccinations
daily exercise
dental hygiene
junk food

General
school teams
cheerleaders
students who break school rules
separate gym classes for boys and
   for girls
school sponsored social events

Troubleshooting the Decision-Making Strategy

Question 1: What Are the Options?

Students don't understand what this question asks them to do. This step is all about brainstorming, a problem-solving technique in which all members of a group contribute ideas without judging them according to their value. (Judging occurs in the next step, when complete reasons are given.) Explain that this question asks them to think about all the things they COULD do, not necessarily the things they SHOULD do. Be strict about it by insisting that students offer creative and unusual ideas as the yardsticks require, and do not allow any comments or judgments until the next step.

Question 2: What Are the Reasons?

This step feels like too much to do. If this step seems like it should be two steps rather than one, you may be stressing the nomination of "promising" options too much. The choice of which options are promising enough to warrant further consideration should be a pretty easy one. Chances are that the majority of your students will agree readily to which options are the most interesting or viable, choose them quickly (perhaps by taking a vote), and be ready to move on. If you guide the nomination process to run a quick and natural course, this step becomes a very manageable one.

However, if the majority of your students disagree on which options are the most promising, the session could disintegrate into an argument over which ones to pursue. Don't give into this pitfall. Split the class into two or more "camps" and let them quickly give reasons for the options of their choice. This is a nice way to demonstrate that there are no "right" or "only" answers for most decision points. It also avoids the problem of bogging down during the nomination of options.

Question 3: What Is the Best Choice?

Students have problems weighing reasons. If weighing reasons is initially difficult or unclear, make it more concrete by assigning numerical values to each reason. Give a "5" to any reasons that seem to be very important and a "1" to reasons that do not seem to be very important. You might also use positive numbers for pros and negative numbers for cons. Then add up the value of all the pros and subtract the value of the cons to find out which option has the highest rating. The option with the highest rating is, of course, the best careful choice.

In General

Students don't have answers to the powerful questions. As awkward as the silences are, wait for answers. Remember that research shows that even a three-second pause can result in an increase in responses from students. Stack papers, walk around the room, or count to ten—do whatever you have to do to give your students time to think and formulate responses. Remember, too, that giving quotas often helps. Ask for a specific number of ideas (three, four, or five) and you are very likely to get them.

Students have too many answers to the powerful questions. If you find that taking every response and writing it on the board takes too much time, there is a way to speed things up without undermining enthusiasm or participation. Simply give fair warning that time is up. Explain that you will take two or three more ideas and then you need to move on. Be sure that you call on each student at some point during the session, but NOT for every question. This will encourage participation and keep things moving at the same time.

Students give inappropriate answers to the questions. Because one purpose of the strategy is to cultivate creative thinking, try not to react at all to silly or unsuitable responses. Do write them on the board, however, as you would any other response. By not reacting negatively, you will be allowing students to feel free to take chances with answers or ideas and you may be pleasantly surprised to find that sometimes the "silly" response generates a good idea. In addition, the inappropriate responses will not get the usual, anticipated attention-getting effect. The exception, of course, is genuine discipline problems which you should deal with as you normally would.

The strategy takes too long. Remember that the time estimates at the beginning of each practice session are realistic. If you find that you are taking much longer and are either pinched for time or are loosing your students' attention, there are several things you can do.

First, try the same approach recommended for situations in which students have too many answers. Set limits on the number of responses you will take and stick to them. Second, try having students work on paper or in groups. Doing this will cut down on the amount of time that you spend calling on students and writing their responses on the board. This will also ensure that everyone stays involved.

If all else fails, you can always trim a lesson down as a last resort. For example, it is better to do just Get Ready, one powerful question, and Think About Thinking than to do nothing at all because of time constraints. Use your best judgment about what to include and what to leave out. You know what your students need to work on most.

The yardsticks are troublesome. The yardsticks are intended to be used as a guide or prompt to extend thinking. If you find that they are becoming a stumbling block, you or your students may be overusing them or using them too literally. Don't worry, for example, about exactly which response fulfills which yardstick. Simply remind students to use the yardsticks if they seem to be unable to move forward with a particular question, or ask them if they have considered the yardsticks, or if the results of their thinking measure up to the yardsticks.

3 | *The Understanding Through Design Strategy*

Module Three: *Overview*

Module Three teaches a systematic, step-by-step way to explore and understand an incredibly wide range of things, which we call "designs." By using this strategy, students will be able to better understand such diverse designs as objects (compasses, covered wagons, or dictionaries, for example), concepts (such as justice, government, or agriculture), and events (such as greetings, Paul Revere's ride, or Thanksgiving Day).

Once again students become involved in searching for thorough and thoughtful answers to three powerful questions:

1. What are the purposes of the design?
2. What are its features and the reasons for them?
3. How well does the design work?

Students will learn to approach each thing to be discussed as a design—something that has both purposes and features or parts. Once they have identified the purposes of the design, they will look at the features and find reasons for them. Finally, students will evaluate the effectiveness of the design.

The Understanding Through Design Strategy can be used alone or as "filler" for the Thinking Sandwich. Using the Mental Management Strategy to begin a lesson with Get Ready and conclude it with Make Connections and/or Think About Thinking will help students strengthen these skills.

In order that both teachers and students become familiar with this strategy, it is suggested that some time almost every day be used to present and practice the strategy for a period of four weeks as outlined below.

Suggested Timetable for Module Three

WEEK 9 Monday: **Orientation Lesson** *(40 minutes)*
Tuesday – Friday: **What Are the Purposes? Practice**
(15 minutes each day)

WEEK 10 Monday – Friday: **What Are the Features and Reasons? Practice** *(20 minutes each day)*

WEEK 11 Monday – Friday: **How Well Does It Work? Practice**
(20 minutes each day)

WEEK 12 Any three days: **Pulling It All Together Practice**
(40 minutes each day)

ORIENTATION LESSON

Purpose of this Lesson

The Orientation Lesson will introduce students to the Understanding Through Design Strategy and give them a general understanding of how the strategy works from beginning to end. It will provide them with a basis upon which they can fine-tune the details of the strategy over the next four weeks.

Learning, practicing, and hopefully mastering this strategy will enable students to become careful evaluators and good critical thinkers now and throughout their lives.

Preparation

- A sample Orientation Lesson that uses the dictionary as a design is provided on the following pages as a model for your use. Read through it to familiarize yourself with the procedures and the key words and phrases used in this strategy. While many of you will find the dictionary a useful design to explore with students, some may prefer to choose another design for this lesson. (See pages 126–127 for other appropriate design suggestions.)

- If you choose to teach the Dictionary Lesson, have available individual dictionaries or enough of them for students to share in a manageable way.

- The Classroom Guide on page 93 provides an abbreviated lesson plan which you may find useful in reviewing your lesson strategy and conducting your lesson.

- Display the Understanding Through Design poster in a prominent place in the classroom.

- All lesson plans in this manual assume that chalkboard and chalk or chart paper and a marker are available to record student responses.

Approximate Classroom Time Needed

WEEK 9 Monday: *40 minutes*

The Dictionary Lesson

1. Direct attention to the poster.

Introduce the Understanding Through Design Strategy by asking a volunteer to read the name of this new strategy as shown on the poster. Tell them that this strategy will enable them to understand all kinds of things better, both in and out of school.

Explain that they will be using the word *design* in this strategy when talking about different kinds of things—things such as objects, concepts or ideas, and even events. Give a few examples to help students understand this. Then go on to explain that a design is anything that has certain parts, or features, in order to do certain things, or serve a purpose. As a quick illustration of a simple design, hold up an ordinary pencil.

Ask, "Can anyone name some purposes of a pencil?" (Possible answers: *Pencils are used to write or draw things; to write and be able to correct mistakes; to be put in compasses; to be read by computers that read standardized test forms.*)

Then suggest that students examine the pencil closely and name some of its features. List all responses on the board or chart paper. (Possible answers: *The pencil is make of wood; it is long and skinny; it has graphite in the center of the wood; it has a rubber tip on one end.*)

Now ask students to consider the features and think of reasons for them. These reasons should serve the purposes of the pencil. (Possible answers: *The pencil is made of wood so that it can easily be sharpened; the wood protects the graphite; it is long and skinny so that it can be held easily or put into a compass; it has graphite to make marks on paper; it has a rubber tip on one end so pencil marks can be erased.*)

2. Present the design to be considered and discuss the first question: What are the purposes of the design?

Tell students that the design for today is the dictionary. Ask them to take a minute or two to Get Ready as you distribute copies of the dictionary. Then ask everyone to look carefully at the dictionary and to notice things about it—especially things they have never noticed before, such as how much it weighs, what it is made of, how it feels, and so on.

After a few minutes, ask students to think about the first powerful question and to name as many purposes of the dictionary as they can. (If necessary, explain that *purpose* means its use.) On the board or chart, record all responses regarding the purposes or uses of the dictionary. (Possible responses: *The purpose of the dictionary is to look up words; it tells how to pronounce words; in the back of it, it tells what abbreviations mean; it's supposed to help you with spelling.*)

The Understanding Through Design Strategy

3. Point out and explain the yardsticks.

Remind students that they have already learned about and used yardsticks in the Decision-Making Strategy. Ask if anyone can explain what they are (*reminders or suggestions for what to think about while answering each question.*) Point to the first of the four yardsticks on the poster. Explain that "key" purposes are the main or major ones. Ask students if they wish to add any key purposes other than the ones already suggested. If so, add them to the list. Then point out that stopping with only the key purposes would skip over or ignore many other different purposes, especially creative purposes and hidden purposes—the ones that aren't always obvious or thought of right away.

Give students a few minutes to think of varied, creative, and hidden purposes. Then add them to the list. (Possible answers: *Some varied purposes could be to learn a foreign language if you had a dictionary with English words and words in another language; there's an index in the back that shows lots of different purposes—everything from "Firsts in Space" to "Learning Signs and Symbols." A creative purpose of a dictionary is that it could be used as a booster seat for little children or as a bookend because it's big and heavy. A hidden purpose might be to make money for the people who sell them—like bookstore owners or publishers.*)

If you find students are struggling with this step, offer prompts as necessary to stimulate their thinking.

4. Discuss the second question: What are the features of the design and the reasons for them?

If necessary, explain that *features* are parts or qualities of the design. Help students to understand that this second powerful question asks them to think about which parts or qualities of the design help serve its purposes. In other words: What is the design made up of, and why? Your classroom discussion of this second question might sound something like this:

Teacher: Now think about the dictionary. What are its features or characteristics?

Student: The words are listed in alphabetical order.

Teacher: Yes, they are. Now can you think of reasons for that feature? Remember the question is, "What are the features AND the reasons for them?"

Student: Well, so you can find the words. It would be really hard to find them if they were just thrown in there.

Teacher: Good. Let me write that down. Can anyone else think of another feature?

Student: The dictionary has definitions in it...so you can find out what words mean.

Teacher: Right. That's how features are related to purposes; they are connected. The parts of a dictionary are there in order to serve the purpose of a dictionary. Any more ideas?

Student: The dictionary is printed with black ink on paper (*Pause.*) Because that's how books are made.

Teacher: Can you elaborate, or give more details, about your reason?

Student: Well, it's because paper is thin, and you can fit a lot in one book. Black ink was probably chosen because it shows up on paper better than other colors.

Student: Another feature is that there are different types of dictionaries: big, huge ones, like I see in libraries, and big ones with hard covers, and smaller ones like paper backs, and even ones that fit in your pocket. I guess that's so everyone can have what they need.

When you feel ready to move on, call attention to the yardsticks for the second question that are listed on the poster. Explain that measuring up to these yardsticks means thinking of features that are physical, organizational, have to do with how the design was made, how it affects people, and so on. It also means being sure to explain how a feature helps the design serve its purpose.

To help students stretch their thinking, say something like: "Another feature might have to do with how the dictionary gets written. Any ideas? Be sure to include reasons!" (Possible responses: *It was probably written by a group of people because a group could do the work much quicker than just one person could; dictionaries cost a lot of money and the reason for that is so the company that made them can make a profit and pay all of their researchers and writers.*)

Record all responses. Comment on whether or not you think the list measures up to the yardsticks and prompt students to think carefully about any ones that are unfulfilled.

5. Discuss the third question: How well does the design work?

Direct attention to the third powerful question on the poster and point out its corresponding yardsticks. Explain that students should now carefully consider all of the features (and reasons) and think about what's good about the dictionary (pros) and what's not good about it (cons).

Ask, "What are some good points, or pro features, of the dictionary?" (Possible responses: *One good thing about the dictionary is that it makes it easy to look up what words mean; once you know how to use phonetic symbols, you can learn how to pronounce words; there's an awful lot of information packed into one book.*)

Then ask, "What are some negative points, or cons, about it?" (Possible responses: *One not so good thing is that the dictionary doesn't really help you with spelling. If you can't spell a word, how can you look it up? Another con is that even the small dictionaries are too big to carry around. It seems like you never have one when you need it.*)

Now challenge students to think of ways in which the design (the dictionary) could be improved. Encourage everyone to participate in the brainstorming. Remind them that there are no right or wrong answers and the point is to make the dictionary more useful. (Possible responses: *Make dictionaries like skinny pocket calculators so people can type in a word and either get a list of possible spellings or the definition. Another idea would be to put dictionaries everywhere—in bus stops, restrooms, hotel rooms, restaurants—so they would always be there when you needed one.*)

Before concluding this lesson, ask students to take a few minutes to do one or both of the post-task steps: Make Connections and Think About Thinking.

6. Review the Understanding Through Design Strategy.

End the lesson by complimenting students on their work and remark that they probably have a better understanding of the dictionary now. Refer to the poster again and briefly review the process that they have just completed.

Explain that in the following weeks everyone will be practicing each step in the strategy, one at a time. Stress that learning to use this strategy will help students become sharp evaluators and better critical thinkers. Encourage everyone to try out this new strategy on something at home. Tell them that you and the class will be interested in hearing about it and extend an invitation for them to talk about their experiences.

Classroom Guide

1. Direct attention to the poster.

Explain the purpose of this strategy and the meaning of the word *design* as used here. To help them understand the concept, ask students to consider the pencil as an example of a simple design. Guide them to discuss the purposes of the pencil and some of its features.

2. Present the design to be considered and discuss the first question: What are the purposes of the design?

Begin by suggesting that students take some time to Get Ready. If you have selected the dictionary (or other object) as the design, show it to the students and have them take a good hard look at it. Ask them to list the purposes or uses of the design you have chosen. Record all responses.

3. Point out and explain the yardsticks.

Bring out that yardsticks are reminders or suggestions for what to think about while answering each powerful question. Give students time to add key purposes and to think of varied, creative, and hidden ones to add to their list.

4. Discuss the second question: What are the features of the design and the reasons for them?

If necessary, explain the meaning of *features*. List all features of the dictionary (or other object) that students suggest. Remind them to give reasons for their suggestions. Have them use the yardsticks to stretch their thinking. Record all suggestions.

5. Discuss the third question: How well does the design work?

Use the yardsticks to guide students to consider both the positive features (the pros) and the negative ones (the cons) of the dictionary (the design) in order to evaluate how well it works. Challenge them to think of ways in which it could be improved. Record all responses. Before concluding the lesson, give students some time to Make Connections and/or Think About their Thinking.

6. Review the Understanding Through Design Strategy.

Conclude by complimenting students and summarizing the main steps of this strategy. Emphasize the importance of this process and the effect it will have on their thinking.

After-the-Lesson Checklist

- Did you give students enough time to carefully examine the design?

- Did you adequately explain the key words and phrases?

- Did you give enough examples of designs, purposes, and features so that students understood the distinctions?

- Did you stress the use of the yardsticks but not so much that they became a roadblock?

- Did you keep the lesson moving and about 40 minutes long?

Teachers' Questions and Authors' Answers

Q: Is it necessary to use words such as *design* and *varied*?

A: We are aware that students may have some difficulty at first with the vocabulary in this strategy. However, there are some words, such as *design, features,* and *varied* that are important to use for several reasons. One is that their definitions are precise, making them difficult to replace with "easier" words. Another extremely important reason is our concern that your students learn the language of thinking, and are equipped with the words they will need to describe their thoughts and thought processes. Because paying attention to, describing, and evaluating their own thinking is probably new to students, they are likely to have some difficulty with a few of the words in these lessons. However, we know that your students can learn them.

You may need to take a few extra minutes to explain words and give some simple examples, or suggest that students look them up in a dictionary. Have the patience to occasionally remind them of the meanings of those difficult words. Some teachers have made the words part of their students' vocabulary lists. You may wish to do this also.

Q: I can think of a few things in the curriculum for which I can use this strategy, but I'm unsure about whether or not they are "designs." How do I know if I'm choosing subjects or topics correctly?

A: Let us assure you that it is hard to choose something that is **NOT** a design. If the topic you would like to teach using this strategy has a purpose (or purposes) as well as parts, events, characteristics, or qualities that serve the purpose(s), it's a design.

As far as we have been able to determine, the only things that do **NOT** work as designs are those things whose features do not serve a specific purpose, such as the orbits of the planets. However, the theories or concepts related to them **ARE** designs because they **DO** serve a purpose— they may explain how something works, for example.

For instance, gravity is not a design, but the theory of gravity is. One obvious purpose of the theory of gravity is to explain why things fall when we let go of them. One obvious feature is that the theory says gravity decreases with distance. Therefore, if you find something that doesn't seem to lend itself to the "purposes" and "features" questions very well, consider using the theory instead.

Purpose of these Practices

One of the most common gaps in the comprehension of many students is the lack of understanding of what things are for; that is, of the purpose of things. This is especially true of subject matter concepts, events, and activities. This practice encourages students to look closely at a number of designs and find their various purposes. By determining in some detail what things are for, students will come to better understand and remember them.

Teachers will learn a quick questioning strategy that will enable students to achieve a deeper understanding of the importance of the things that they are learning. This week students will focus on answering only the first question in this strategy: What are the purposes of the design?

Preparation

- Display the Understanding Through Design poster in a prominent place in the classroom.

- Read through the Classroom Guide on the next page.

- Identify four places in your curriculum where students can practice this step and choose an appropriate design for each. Use any concept, object, or event as long as it is designed to serve one or more purposes. Record these subjects and designs in the Weekly Planner on page 121. Some possibilities are:

Science	What are the purposes of a birds' nest?
Language Arts	What are the purposes of the alphabet?
Social Studies	What are the purposes of the concept of equality?
Mathematics	What are the purposes of the metric system?
General	What are the purposes of computers?

(See pages 126–127 for additional suggestions.)

- If you use any objects as designs in these lessons, try to provide an example of it for students to examine and handle, or at least provide a picture of it. If the object is not available or if the design is abstract, give a detailed verbal description of it.

- Use the Working Outline on page 122 to make notes, recommendations, or changes in your daily lesson plans.

Approximate Classroom Time Needed

WEEK 9   Tuesday – Friday: *15 minutes each day*

Classroom Guide

1. Direct attention to the poster.

Help students recall their experience with previewing the Understanding Through Design Strategy and tell them that they will become better at using this strategy after they have had more practice answering each of the questions. Suggest that students take a minute now to Get Ready.

2. Present the design to be considered today.

If you have chosen an abstract idea to use as the design, give students a complete description or example of it. If you have chosen an object, pass it around and have students examine it carefully. Remind everyone to think about what this design is for as they consider it.

3. Discuss the first question: What are the purposes of the design?

Ask students to name as many purposes of the design as they can. Record all responses, forming a list on the board or chart. Remember not to pass judgment on any of the responses while acting as the recorder. A casual "all right" or "okay" is all that is necessary as an acknowledgment.

4. Call attention to the yardsticks on the poster.

Have students recall what is meant by *key, varied, creative,* and *hidden* purposes. Ask students to decide if their list measures up to these yardsticks and includes examples of the various purposes. If not, give them a few more minutes to think, then add any additional suggestions to the list.

5. Conclude the practice.

Suggest that everyone take some time to do one or both of the post-task steps, Make Connections or Think About Thinking. Afterward, compliment students on their work and summarize what they have achieved during this practice. Emphasize the usefulness of this process by pointing out that they now have a much more thorough understanding of the design after thoughtfully reviewing all of its purposes.

Note: Save the lists of purposes for each design that students generate during the practices this week. You may wish to use them during the other steps of this strategy. If you used the chalkboard to record responses, have a volunteer copy the lists at the end of each session.

A Classroom Example

You have decided to use the abstract idea, *Education*, as the design for today. Your practice session might develop something like this:

Teacher: Today I'd like you to think about elementary school education. Let's start with the first question on the poster. What are some of the purposes of elementary education? By that I mean, what is elementary education for? Take a few minutes now to Get Ready for this task. (*After a minute or two of silence, the teacher writes "Purposes of Education" on the board or chart.*) Any ideas about what education is for?

Student: It's so we learn things.

Teacher: Okay. Any other ideas? (*Begins a numbered list and writes in the first response.*)

Student: Another purpose is to get us ready for jobs when we're older.

Teacher: All right, I'll add that to the list. Anyone else?

No further suggestions are offered. After a minute, the teacher directs attention to the poster and the yardsticks. Together, teacher and students decide that the purposes given so far are key ones. There aren't any varied, creative, or hidden purposes listed, so they decide that they must continue to think.

Student: It gives us a place to go while our parents work.

Student: It's to bore us to death!

While everyone giggles, the teacher writes both responses without reacting, then mentions another purpose to prompt more ideas.

Teacher: How about this: another purpose is to teach you how to get along with each other.

Student: Maybe a hidden purpose is to provide people with jobs, like teachers and janitors and all.

Student: And maybe it's just to keep us busy and out of the work force for a few years.

Student: A really important purpose is to teach us to think better.

The teacher completes the list and asks the class to recheck to see if they measured up to the yardsticks. Then the teacher suggests that students Think About their Thinking. After a moment or two, the teacher concludes the lesson.

After-the-Lesson Checklist

- Did students understand the meaning of *purposes*?
- Did you give students time to think by turning away, walking around the room, or other tactics?
- Did you avoid reacting negatively to answers?
- Did you use prompts only if they were needed?
- Did the practice last only about 15 minutes?

Teachers' Questions and Authors' Answers

Q: How do I help my students look at the purposes of a design from different angles?

A: Looking at something from a fresh viewpoint can be tough at first, but student do get better at it with practice. Try using some of the questions below to help them really probe the purposes of a design in depth:

- Who uses the design and for what purposes? (For example: Who uses vitamins? Why? Who listens to the National Anthem? Why?)

- If the design was made by humans, why was it made? (For example: Why was the protractor made?)

- If the design was developed by nature, what factors in the environment might have contributed to its development? (For example: What does an eggshell do for an egg?)

- Who contributes or contributed to the design and why? (For example: Who contributes to archaeology? Why?)

- Where is the design found? For what purposes? (For example: Where is zero found? Why?)

Q: I still have trouble finding time to do these practices even though I know they are important. How can I fit them into my already full day?

A: Even though this program infuses the teaching of thinking skills into your regular lessons, it does take time. And perhaps it takes additional classroom time for you. That means that something you are doing now will have to be given less time. Think of the most important content that you teach. It is this content that deserves emphasis. That is where these strategies should be used. Spending the time—or extra time—will ensure that your students get more than a superficial, short-lived understanding of the material.

Another reminder: Be sure that you don't spend unnecessary time slavishly categorizing students' responses by the yardstick measures. Instead, merely ask, "Are all of the yardstick covered?" or "Does your list measure up to the yardsticks?"

Q: This seems too easy. I set up designs for students and then facilitate their working in groups. They're doing the work; I'm not. Am I doing enough?

A: By acting as manager and facilitator, you allow students to become actively involved in their own learning instead of being passive learners. After all, students do learn better if they are the ones actually doing the work. You are doing more than enough. Keep up the good work!

WHAT ARE THE FEATURES AND REASONS? *Practices*

Purpose of these Practices

Knowing what a design is made of and why is a fundamental part of understanding that design. This week students will thoroughly explore what the particular design that they are considering is made up of; in other words, they will identify the features of the design. They will also consider why the design has these features; in other words, they will identify the reasons for those features. In addition to the obvious features, students will learn to recognize features that many people might ordinarily overlook—and explore the reasons for them.

Preparation

■ Display the Understanding Through Design poster in a prominent place in the classroom.

■ Read through the Classroom Guide on the next page.

■ Identify five places in your curriculum for the upcoming week in which students can practice this step and choose an appropriate design for each. Record these subjects and designs in the Weekly Planner on page 121. Some possibilities are:

Health	The circulatory system: What are the features of this system and the reasons for them?
Mathematics	Problem solving: What are the features of problem solving and the reasons for them?
Reading	A short story: What are the features of a short story and for what reasons?
Social Studies	A physical map: What are the features of a map and for what reasons?
Science	Plant roots: What are the features of roots and the reasons for them?
General	A chapter review: What are the features of the review and reasons for them?

(See pages 126–127 for additional suggestions.)

■ Use the Working Outline on page 123 to make notes, recommendations, or changes in your daily lesson plans.

Approximate Classroom Time Needed

WEEK 10 Monday – Friday: *20 minutes each day*

Classroom Guide

1. Direct attention to the poster.

Explain that each day this week, everyone will spend some time concentrating on the second powerful question in this strategy. Ask a volunteer to quickly review the point of looking for the purposes of a design. Then ask everyone to take a moment to Get Ready for today's practice session.

2. Present the design to be considered today.

Take time to introduce the design so that everyone understands it. This is especially important if you have chosen an abstract idea, such as a concept or an event. If you have chosen an object, pass it around and give students time to examine it. Remind everyone to think about the features, or parts of this design.

3. Discuss the second question: What are the features of the design and the reasons for them?

Invite students to suggest as many features, or parts, or characteristics of the design as they can. Remind them to give reasons for their suggestions. If they suggest features but do not address the reasons for them, ask "Why?" or "For what reasons?" to prompt their full responses. Acknowledge all responses nonjudgmentally as you record them.

4. Remind students to use the yardsticks.

Without belaboring the point, remind them of the yardsticks listed on the poster and that they are there to help stretch their thinking. Ask students to think of different kinds of features and the reasons for those features, or how the features help the design serve its purposes.

5. Conclude the practice.

Have students do the Make Connections and/or Think About Thinking step. Afterward, compliment students on their thoughtful work and summarize today's practice. Each day this week, emphasize how learning to answer this question helps students understand the design and explore the topic they are studying more fully.

Note: Save the lists that students generate during the practices this week as you may wish to use them later in this strategy. If you used the chalkboard to record responses, have a volunteer copy the lists at the end of each session.

A Classroom Example

You have decided to use the on-line computer card catalog as the design for today. Your practice session might develop something like this:

Teacher: Today you're going to listen to the librarian explain the on-line computer card catalog. As you are listening, please think about the features of this card catalog and reasons for those features. I think you will find it helpful to make notes to use during our class discussion later. Now before you leave for the library, let's take a minute now to Get Ready.

The teacher ends the quiet time by dismissing students and reminding them to look for features of the computer card catalog and the reasons for them. When students return to the classroom, the teacher continues.

Teacher: Can someone name a feature or part of the computer card catalog and the reasons for it?

Student: There's a record in the computer of every book in the library.

Teacher: Yes, that's a feature, but what are the reasons for that feature?

Student: So you can find the book you want quickly.

Many students seem anxious to contribute. To save time, the teacher decides not to write the responses on the board and sets a limit of five more responses.

Student: Another feature is that you can input the name of the author, subject, title, or a key word. The reason for that is so you can find what you want even if you only know one thing, like the subject or part of the title.

Students offer a few suggestions, but they question whether or not they are meeting the standards of the yardstick.

Teacher: Yardsticks are reminders, not rigid rules. They are there to help you stretch your thinking. Just ask yourself, "Have I tried to think about the computer card catalog not just in obvious ways, but also in unusual ways?"

The teacher walks around the room or turns away from the class to give them time to think.

Student: If you call up the author's name, all the titles of books by that author show up on the screen. They are listed alphabetically under the author's last name. That's a feature. The reason is that it makes it easy to find other books by a favorite author.

Teacher: The computer card catalog also shows which public libraries have the book you want, so that the librarian can quickly get it if it's not in the school library.

The teacher asks for a few other suggestions and then moves on to Make Connections. Students connect the information about the computer card catalog to the dictionary and to the phone book, as both are also organized to allow people to find things quickly. Then students connect the process of learning about the card catalog to learning how to use a calculator or a personal computer. During Think About Thinking, students comment on how hard it was to remember everything because there's so much to learn in order to use the on-line card catalog. The teacher concludes the session.

After-the-Lesson Checklist

- If the design was an object, did you give students an example of it to examine? If the design was abstract, did you describe it well and give a specific example?

- Did students give reasons for the features they mentioned? If not, did you prompt them to do so?

- Did students remember to use the yardsticks? If not, did you remind them to do so?

- Did you reinforce the value of learning this strategy at the end of the lesson?

Teachers' Questions and Authors' Answers

Q: What should I do when students give wild or inappropriate responses or comments that are strictly attention-getters?

A: When students give the type of responses that you described, they are probably testing you. Pass the test by not reacting. Just write their responses on the board. If you play a neutral role, the attention-getting behaviors will decrease and students will become more serious about the lesson. When you get silly or violent ideas, you could also use the lesson to help you manage things. For example, the yardsticks guide students to think of different kinds of features. Therefore, if students seem to be stuck in a weird frame of mind, remind them that you have acknowledged or written several of their ideas, but now they need to come up with DIFFERENT KINDS of features. Of course, if you have a discipline problem, handle it as you usually would.

Q: I am still standing in front of the room leading most of the lessons. I feel that every time I give up a little control, the whole thing falls apart. What do you suggest?

A: As you know, every class is different. In general, though, most classes are not accustomed to being given responsibility for the lesson, so they will tend to go to pieces—at first. Therefore, it is very important that you relinquish control in stages. Be sure to communicate your expectations to the students. For example, you might begin by having students work independently, then have some take on the role of recorder, then have them work in groups to share ideas, and so on. Rather than just suddenly stepping aside, think of giving your students more autonomy little by little. Gradually move from being the leader to being an assistant, then to being a guide or facilitator and eventually to becoming a resource person.

During this process of encouraging students to think independently, perhaps the most valuable trait you can manifest is a tolerance for their awkwardness! You must be able to endure the long silences that ensue when students are thinking or when they are stuck and hope that you will pull them out. You must resist the urge to continue a wonderful discussion when you know it should be cut off. You must come to terms with these feelings as you slowly and gently give your students control over their own thinking.

Purpose of these Practices

In this third and final step of the Understanding Through Design Strategy, students will think critically and creatively about an object, concept, or event. As they consider the design, they will ask themselves the third powerful question: How well does it work?

This is an important step for students as they will learn to evaluate the pros and cons in order to decide how well the features serve the purposes of the design. Then students will be asked to imagine how the design might be improved. To do this, they must consider which aspects of the design can be changed and which cannot, in order to think of creative but realistic possibilities for improvements.

Preparation

■ Display the Understanding Through Design poster in a prominent place in the classroom.

■ Read through the Classroom Guide on the next page.

■ Identify five places in your curriculum for the upcoming week where students can practice this step. Consider using designs that have been discussed in the previous practices for this strategy. Record these subjects and designs in the Weekly Planner on page 121. Other possibilities are:

Science	Pollution controls: How well do they work?
Social Studies	Democracy: How well does it work in the United States?
Mathematics	Circle graphs: How well do they work?

(See pages 126–127 for additional suggestions.)

■ If you choose to use them, have copies of The Strategy Worksheet or Checklist on pages 119–120 to give to your students (one for each group recorder or one for each student if students are working alone).

■ Use the Working Outline on page 124 to make notes, recommendations, or changes in your daily lesson plans.

Approximate Classroom Time Needed

WEEK 11 Monday – Friday: *20 minutes each day*

Classroom Guide

1. Direct attention to the poster.

Ask volunteers to quickly review this strategy and the first two powerful questions that have been practiced. Explain that this week the class will be focusing on the third powerful question in this strategy. Before you begin, suggest that everyone take some quiet time to Get Ready.

2. Present the design to be considered today.

Take time to introduce the design so that everyone understands it. If the design is an object, have an example of it, if at all possible, for students to examine. If the design is abstract, describe it thoroughly and offer specific examples.

3. Review the purposes of the design, as well as the features and reasons for them.

If you are using a design from a previous practice session, quickly review the design's purposes, and the features and reasons that have been previously discussed. If you are introducing a new design today, quickly build the necessary background for it.

4. Discuss the third question: How well does the design work?

Consider having students work in small groups to discuss this question. To do this, guide the formation of workable groups and suggest that a volunteer in each group be the recorder. If volunteers are not forthcoming, appoint ones.

Remind the class of any rules you have established for small groups and help them focus by calling attention to the yardsticks listed for this question on the poster. Tell students to consider the first one and take some time to evaluate the design by considering pros and cons, then think about improvements. Encourage realistic as well as unusual and creative ideas. Circulate among the groups offering assistance or prompts only as needed.

5. Conclude the practice.

Encourage students to do the Make Connections and/or the Think About Thinking step. Afterward, compliment them on their work. Summarize the highlights of today's session and emphasize how answering this question will help students become stronger critical and creative thinkers.

A Classroom Example

The class has been studying European geography and you decide to use European national boundaries as the design for today. Your practice session might develop something like this:

The teacher talks briefly about the purposes of boundaries and some of their features and reasons. She or he has elected to have students work in small groups and gives a Strategy Worksheet to the student in each group who will act as the recorder.

Teacher: Notice the third question on the poster and its yardsticks. First think of as many pros and cons for national boundaries as you can. Then we'll meet as a class to discuss them. If you need help, I'm here.

The teacher walks around the room as students work, offering encouragement and praise. After students have worked up a good intellectual sweat, the teacher asks them to gather together again as a class.

Teacher: What were some of your more interesting pros and cons for the boundaries?

Student: Our group had lots of cons. One is that people fight over borders. Another is that the border guards can take a long time to check you through when you want to cross boundaries.

Student: But that's a pro, too. Border guards check for illegal things so they help keep countries safe.

Teacher: Yes, that's okay. A feature can have BOTH a pro and a con associated with it.

Students give a few more responses and the teacher decides to move on in order to keep the lesson under twenty minutes.

Teacher: Now how about improvements? Please form your groups again to brainstorm ideas. Then choose one improvement to share when the class meets in about five minutes.

Afterwards, the teacher calls the class together and invites a spokesperson from each group to share an improvement.

Student: We decided that people who live near borders should be allowed to vote for whichever country they choose to call their own country. That way, there might be less fighting.

Student: We thought the boundaries should be in places where people don't live—the jungle or high in the mountains—so people wouldn't fight about them.

Student: People would fight about them no matter where they are. We thought there should just not be boundaries in Europe. When you think about it, it could work.

Teacher: You came up with some interesting suggestions. In reality, Europe is working to break down some of its boundaries—not national ones, but economic ones. Thanks for your hard work today. It paid off in some really good ideas. In fact it gives me another idea. National boundaries remind me of school boundaries. How do you suppose it would be if we broke down the boundaries between grade levels? We might use that concept as a design for another day.

After-the-Lesson Checklist

- Did you make sure students used the worksheets correctly?

- Did students understand that they were to evaluate how well the design worked, that is, how well its features served its purposes?

- Did you encourage students to think of both pros and cons?

- Did you refrain from passing judgment or reacting negatively to suggestions that were not realistic?

Teachers' Questions and Authors' Answers

Q: How can my students evaluate how well the features of a design serve its purposes, or how can they imagine improvements if they don't know what the features or purposes are?

A: If your students already have a good understanding of or feel for the design, they will jump right in with pros and cons. However, if you use a design that hasn't been explored in any way or in a previous session, you will need to mention a few purposes of the design, as well as features and the reasons for them, or quickly have the class build this background, before you can address this "how well does it work" question.

Keep in mind, however, that there are no hard and fast rules. You may also find yourself using the evaluation question FIRST, then backing up to look at some purposes, and features and reasons if the direct approach doesn't work.

Q: Sometimes my students' suggestions for improvements in a design are outlandish. How realistic should I insist their ideas for improvements be?

A: Although it is important to encourage your students' imagination, it is also important to anchor their thinking in reality. When they give what seems to be far-fetched suggestions, ask them to expand on their suggestion by explaining how they would go about doing or making that improvement. This will allow students to discover unrealistic suggestions for themselves and perhaps prompt them to think more creatively and critically, thus coming up with a better, more realistic idea.

PULLING IT ALL TOGETHER

Purpose of these Practices

The practice sessions this week will give students many opportunities to fit together the three questions that they have been working on over the past three weeks. They will also be encouraged to work more independently than they have in the past—a tactic intended to grant students a certain amount of autonomy and encourage them to demonstrate their skill in using this strategy.

Teachers will also have opportunities to step back and enjoy "watching" students think. It will be important for teachers to keep things moving this week, while allowing students to direct their own work, yet making sure that the strategy is being used correctly. This balance is delicate, but you no doubt have a more relaxed feeling about the process by now. You will also find that your students have also gained a certain amount of skill in using this process and will require less direction.

Preparation

- Display the Understanding Through Design poster in a prominent place in the classroom.

- Read through the Classroom Guide on the next page.

- Decide which three days this week you will have students practice using the complete strategy. Identify three places in your curriculum and choose an appropriate design for each. Try to select designs that will provide students with feelings of success when using this strategy. Record the subjects and designs you have chosen in your Weekly Planner. Some possibilities are:

Art	abstract art
Health	the Heimlich maneuver
Music	song lyrics
Reading	a dramatic reading of a play
Science	chlorophyll

  (See pages 126–127 for additional suggestions.)

- Think through how each lesson might unfold. Use the Working Outline on page 125 for any notes about modeling, prompt questions, or reminders that you might use.

- Have copies of the Understanding Through Design Checklist on page 120 to give to your students.

Approximate Classroom Time Needed

WEEK 12 Any three days: *40 minutes each day*

Classroom Guide

1. Present the design for students to consider.

If possible, show students an example or picture of the design. If the design is abstract, describe it well and give specific examples. Allow some time for students to examine the design or ask questions about it. Remind everyone of the Thinking Sandwich and the Mental Management Strategy. Then suggest that students take a moment to Get Ready for today's task— using the complete Understanding Through Design Strategy.

2. Explain how students should carry out this practice.

Pass out the Checklists for this strategy and encourage students to use them. Assure students that the purpose of the Checklists is to guide them through the steps of the strategy and explain that you'd like them to do the strategy pretty much on their own this week. Remind them to carefully answer each of the three powerful questions and to decide when they've measured up to the yardsticks. Point out that you will offer assistance if it is needed.

Have students work as a class, in groups, or individually as you prefer. While students are working, watch and listen and move around the room as they work. Refrain from making corrections or suggestions unless you feel that it is absolutely necessary. By the end of the week, you should be doing very little intervention.

3. Give students time to work.

Give students about 25 minutes to work, saving about 5 to 10 minutes at the end for students to share highlights. Don't go over the details of each step; rather, ask students if they want to share anything that was especially interesting. As a prompt, you might encourage them to share their most promising suggestions for improving the design. Thank volunteers for their contributions and remember not to pass judgment on any of the responses.

4. Conclude the practice.

Congratulate students on their independence and hard work. Briefly summarize what was done today and remind them to use this strategy often. Emphasize that using this strategy will help them understand and remember almost anything better, and it will enable them to become strong critical thinkers.

A Classroom Example

You have decided to use the task of checking math calculations as the design for today. Your practice session begins by giving students a specific example and might develop something like this:

Teacher: Remember the quiz you had last week on long division? I reminded you beforehand to check your work, but I'm not sure that everyone gave it enough thought. So today I'd like you to use checking your math problems as the design to think about. Please take a minute or so to Get Ready first.

The teacher gives students a few moments of silence and passes out the Checklists for this strategy.

Teacher: Now use the Checklists I have given you as you work through the strategy. Think about the purposes of checking your work...

Student: Checking over our work is supposed to help us catch our mistakes.

There's a long period of silence.

Student: Maybe it's supposed to make us learn from our mistakes, so we don't make them again. Sometimes I make the same dumb mistakes over and over!

Student: Maybe a hidden purpose is to make us slow down when we take a quiz.

Student: I'll bet another hidden one is to make each quiz easier for the teacher to correct since we already corrected most of our mistakes.

Student: Okay, we have to think of features and the reasons for them now. One feature is to go back over our work and the reason is to see if it's right.

Student: Another feature like that one is going over the work carefully so you're not wasting time.

Student: You have to do the figuring again because if you don't, it can look okay but there can be mistakes.

The teacher lets the class discussion continue for a time and then suggests that they move on to the next step.

Student: A pro for the "How Well Does It Work" Question is that if you get the right answers you get good grades.

Student: A con is that usually I don't have enough time to DO everything again.

Student: Another pro is that I'll do the math more carefully the first time since I know that I'll have to fix it later if I work too fast or don't concentrate.

Student: An improvement would be to be given more time so we can take the quiz and check the problems, too.

Student: Another improvement would be to check each other's work before we hand in our papers. That way we'll be sure to check carefully and also try to do good work at first!

The teacher thanks everyone for their contributions and concludes the lesson by suggesting that students Make Connections and Think About Thinking. Students connect checking their work in Math to all their other classes as well as doing chores at home. They think that thinking about the concept was hard, but that it really made them realize how important it is.

After-the-Lesson Checklist

- Did you suggest an interesting and meaningful design for students to work with?

- Did you allow students to work without your help as much as possible?

- Did students have a good grasp of the strategy or did you discover weak areas that need more guidance?

- Did you conclude with a brief review, congratulate students on their work, and remind them of the importance of what they are doing?

Teachers' Questions and Authors' Answers

Q: My students and I have spent twelve weeks learning the three strategies. What do I do now?

A: Congratulations on your hard work and dedication. The most difficult part is over—but the process should continue. It is important that you keep these thinking skills alive by incorporating them into your teaching methods and continuing to infuse them into your regular curriculum. Be sure to reinforce the message that using thinking strategies is something that all of us should do routinely—when working alone, in pairs, with groups, outside of the classroom—throughout our lives.

Use the entire Decision-Making Strategy or Understanding Through Design Strategy with any lessons that you consider to be very important. We suggest that you also do mini-lessons using one powerful question along with the Mental Management Strategy at appropriate times. Mini-lessons are quick, maybe even spontaneous, versions of the "one powerful question" lessons that you have used extensively throughout the twelve weeks. Here are a few examples of times when you might use such mini-lessons:

■ During a lesson using microscopes, you notice that students are awkward in their handling of the instruments. Ask students the "Features and Reasons" Question.

■ The class is about to begin a unit on the moon project that began in the 1960s. You decide to use the Mental Management Strategy along with the "What Are the Purposes" Question from time to time as students progress through the unit. Have students Get Ready, then ask them to write three purposes for exploring the moon. Have students put their papers in their notebooks and save them. Next, ask them to Make Connections and Think About Thinking, even though their responses may be a little lean.

During the last lesson of the unit, ask students to take out their list of purposes, consider the yardsticks, add three more purposes to the list, and share them with the class. Students then do Make Connections and Think About Thinking again. This time they compare their earlier thinking with the thinking that they are doing now.

■ In Social Studies, the class has been studying the settling of the West. Midway through the unit, you decide to challenge students' imagination by using the "How Well Did It Work" Question in connection with covered wagons. During Get Ready, ask students to imagine what it would be like to build a covered wagon, and to ride and to live in one. Then ask students to work in groups to consider how well covered wagons worked. Remind them to think of pros and cons as well as realistic improvements.

Tell students that they should be able to explain in writing or by a drawing how they would improve the covered wagon and why the improvements were needed. (If you wish to impose constraints, such as only using resources that would be available to early settlers, do so.) The pictures and written descriptions may turn out to be so interesting that students arrange them in a bulletin board display.

We hope this gives you a few ideas to consider. In general, you should feel free to be creative and continue to use the strategies to make your classroom truly a thinking one.

Q: How often should I do a thinking activity to keep the Mental Management, Decision-Making, and Understanding Through Design strategies alive in my students' minds?

A: We recommend that you use a thinking activity—any of the three strategies either as a whole or in part—at least once a day, and ideally two or three times a day if you are working with the same students. Remember that these activities can be very brief.

We also recommend that you plan ahead in order to facilitate regular, daily use of thinking activities. Make brief notes about subjects and topics or tasks that your students will be working with for a period of time; perhaps a week. Then decide which strategy or isolated steps of the strategies that you would like students to think through as they study a topic or perform a task. The Sample Planner on pages ix–x in the Introduction of this manual provides an excellent example of how you might do some advance planning.

TEACHER RESOURCES

Contents and Notes

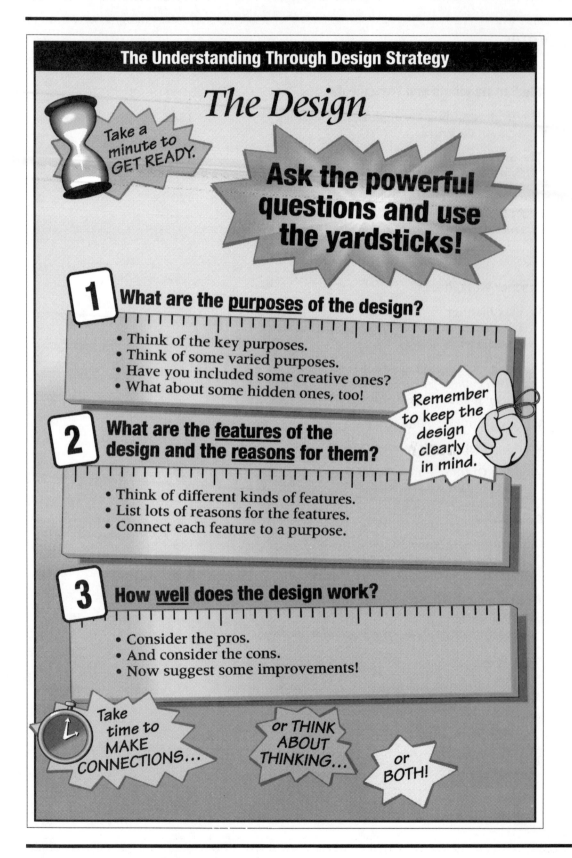

The Understanding Through Design Strategy

The Design

Take a minute to GET READY.

Ask the powerful questions and use the yardsticks!

1 What are the <u>purposes</u> of the design?

- Think of the key purposes.
- Think of some varied purposes.
- Have you included some creative ones?
- What about some hidden ones, too!

Remember to keep the design clearly in mind.

2 What are the <u>features</u> of the design and the <u>reasons</u> for them?

- Think of different kinds of features.
- List lots of reasons for the features.
- Connect each feature to a purpose.

3 How <u>well</u> does the design work?

- Consider the pros.
- And consider the cons.
- Now suggest some improvements!

Take time to MAKE CONNECTIONS...

or THINK ABOUT THINKING...

or BOTH!

The Understanding Through Design Strategy Worksheet

The Design:

Get Ready: Pause...Remember...Imagine...

1. What are the purposes of the design?
Circle the KEY purposes.

_____   _____

_____   _____

_____   _____

2. What are the features of the design and the reasons for them?

Features   *Reasons*

_____   _____

_____   _____

_____   _____

_____   _____

3. How well does the design work?

Pros   *Cons*

_____   _____

_____   _____

_____   _____

_____   _____

Improvements: _____

_____

_____

Make Connections
What does this remind you of? _____

Think About Thinking
What went well? _____

What was hard? _____

What can be improved? _____

The Understanding Through Design Checklist

Make sure to...
- record ALL ideas.
- do every step.
- always use the yardsticks.

If you are working in a group, make sure that...
- everyone participates.
- there is NO criticism of the ideas of others.

The Design:

Get Ready
❏ *Pause.*   ❏ *Remember.*   ❏ *Imagine.*

1. Purposes of the Design
As you think of different kinds of purposes, list them. Use the yardsticks!
- ❏ KEY purposes
- ❏ varied purposes
- ❏ creative purposes
- ❏ hidden purposes

2. Features and Reasons for Them
- ❏ different kinds of features
- ❏ many reasons connecting the features to the purposes

3. How Well Does the Design Work?
- ❏ pros AND cons
- ❏ improvements

❏ *Make Connections*   ❏ *Think About Thinking*

WEEK 9: ORIENTATION LESSON & WHAT ARE THE PURPOSES? PRACTICES

MONDAY	TUESDAY	WEDNESDAY	THURSDAY	FRIDAY
Orientation Lang Arts: the Dictionary	*Purposes Practice* Subject & Design Sandwich Step(s):	*Purposes Practice* Subject & Design Sandwich Step(s):	*Purposes Practice* Subject & Design Sandwich Step(s):	*Purposes Practice* Subject & Design Sandwich Step(s):

WEEK 10: WHAT ARE THE FEATURES AND REASONS? PRACTICES

MONDAY	TUESDAY	WEDNESDAY	THURSDAY	FRIDAY
Subject & Design Sandwich Step(s):	Subject & Design Sandwich Step(s):	Subject & Design Sandwich Step(s):	Subject & Design Sandwich Step(s)	Subject & Design Sandwich Step(s):

WEEK 11: HOW WELL DOES IT WORK? PRACTICES

MONDAY	TUESDAY	WEDNESDAY	THURSDAY	FRIDAY
Subject & Design Sandwich Step(s):	Subject & Design Sandwich Step(s):	Subject & Design Sandwich Step(s):	Subject & Design Sandwich Step(s)	Subject & Design Sandwich Step(s):

WEEK 12: PULLING IT ALL TOGETHER

MONDAY	TUESDAY	WEDNESDAY	THURSDAY	FRIDAY
Subject & Design Sandwich Step(s):		Subject & Design Sandwich Step(s):		Subject & Design Sandwich Step(s):

Working Outline: What Are the Purposes?

1. Direct attention to the poster. Suggest that students spend a minute of quiet time to Get Ready.

2. Present the design to be considered and if possible, allow time for them to examine it. If the design is a concept, provide a description and specific examples.

3. Discuss the first question: What are the purposes of the design?

4. Call attention to the yardsticks on the poster and brainstorm key, varied, creative, and hidden purposes.

5. Conclude with Make Connections and/or Think About Thinking. Praise students for their work and briefly review today's session.

1. Call attention to the poster and the second question. Allow some quiet time to Get Ready.

2. Present the design to be considered and briefly review the purposes of it.

3. Discuss the second question: What are the features and the reasons for them? Prompt students, if necessary, to give reasons for each feature suggested.

4. Remind students to use the yardsticks to stretch their thinking.

5. Conclude with Make Connections and/or Think About Thinking. Praise students for their work and briefly review today's session.

Working Outline: How Well Does It Work?

1. Call attention to the poster and briefly review the first two steps of this strategy. Give students some time to Get Ready.

2. Present the design to be considered.

3. Review the purposes of the design, as well as the features and the reasons for them.

4. Discuss the third question: How well does the design work? Consider having students use the Strategy Worksheets and work in small discussion groups.

5. Conclude with Make Connections and/or Think About Thinking. Praise students for their work and briefly review today's session.

Working Outline: **Pulling It All Together**

1. Present the design for students to consider. Provide a concrete example if possible, or a verbal one. Suggest that students take a moment to Get Ready.

2. Pass out copies of the Checklist and explain that students should use it to work through the steps of the strategy on their own. Offer assistance only as needed.

3. Invite volunteers to share highlights and/or suggestions for improving the design.

4. Conclude with praise and a reminder of the importance of using this strategy.

The Understanding Through Design Strategy can be applied to any "design" that has purposes and features, parts, or characteristics that serve those purposes. The list below offers some suggestions for places in the curriculum where you might use an isolated question (What are the purposes? What are the features and reasons? How well does it work?) or the whole strategy. You will find that you have many more ideas for designs that are specific to your classes. Expand and adapt this list for future use. Be sure to share and exchange ideas with other teachers.

Language Arts
card catalog
business letter
book jacket
diary
comic book
limerick
book report
librarian

Mathematics
number line
abacus
computer
calculator
zero
short cuts in computation
ratio and proportion
mathematician

Science
feathers
weight scales
Natural Science Museum
egg
batteries
hot-air balloons
thermometer
magnifying glass
vitamin tablets
stethoscope
soap
toothbrush
circulatory system
heart as a pump
scales on fish/snakes
scientist
school nurse

Social Studies
Liberty Bell
Japanese tea ceremony
reunification of Germany
National Guard
coins
flags
Congress
primary sources
helmets
crowns
maps
socialism
apartheid
junta
sociologist
historian
physical maps

Art

finger paints
diorama
palette
film
scissors
crayons
art museum
monument
artist or sculptor

Music

instrument
tuning
practice
melody
musical theater
director
vocalist
amplification

Physical Education

team sports
marathons
calisthenics
folk dancing
equipment
sports fans
team spirit

General

friendship
deceptive advertising
kindness
homework
recess
shovel
detention
secrets
cliques
grades
vacations
sharing
animation
competition
photography
fair play
film development
team spirit
brainstorming
memorizing
listening
family trees
courtesy
jails
lockers
book bags
bicycles

Troubleshooting the Understanding Through Design Strategy

Question 1: What Are the Purposes?

Students give only obvious or outrageous purposes. The rules of brainstorming always apply to the thinking process, so accept your students' answers to this question without comment. Remind them, however, that they need to attend to the yardsticks and prompt them to add key purposes and different kinds of purposes to the list. You may want to participate by adding a few unusual purposes yourself. Modeling for them in this manner will help them learn to go beyond the obvious or outrageous responses themselves.

Question 2: What Are the Features and Reasons?

Students will name features, but not reasons. Do not accept responses about the features of the design without the reasons for them. Simply prompt students to give reasons by asking for them. You could also help stimulate their thinking by asking questions such as: Why does the design have that feature? or, How does that feature connect to the purpose of the design?

Don't worry if several features seem to lump together around one reason. Even when this happens, it is still important to mention that one reason for the different features.

Different kinds of features seem hard to find. Try to focus on looking at different DIMENSIONS of a feature, such as tangible and intangible, practical and aesthetic, local and distant, and so on. For example, aside from the physical features of the Egyptian pyramids, there are also less obvious features, such as the ease or difficulty with which they are broken into, their symmetry, their interior dryness or dampness.

Question 3: How Well Does It Work?

Students don't give many pros and cons. As we have mentioned before, when students don't readily respond, give them enough time to think, or set quotas, or both. It is also important to provide prompts when students are first using the process, as well as doing some modeling yourself. This evaluation step is an important one, especially for a "common" or popular design which may otherwise not be fairly or completely evaluated. Be sure to ask for cons and give this as much time as the pro responses.

Students give impractical ideas for improvements. As we have pointed out previously, inappropriate responses are to be accepted and not given any more attention than other responses. In this case, however, you might help students clarify their thinking by encouraging them to explain exactly HOW their improvements might be implemented. If the suggestions are too unrealistic or magical, students are likely to come to this conclusion themselves as they have a hard time explaining how to make it work. Eventually students will give up on offering nonsensical suggestions or they will think them through enough on their own to turn them into practical ones.

In General

Designs are hard to find. Remember that designs can be almost anything made by man or nature—objects, concepts, events, even organizations. All that is needed is that it has some purposes and can be described by features, parts, or characteristics. Consider the suggestions offered in the lesson plans as well as those included in "Opportunities in Your Daily Curriculum" in the Teacher Resources section. You could also talk to other teachers, look around your classroom, flip through your textbooks or newspapers for ideas.

My lessons feel unfocused. If you have chosen a design that is too general or that doesn't really fit the requirements of a design, using the strategy will be difficult. Some examples of poor design choices include natural things that do not have the necessary features-fit-purposes, or the form-follows-function qualifications, like snowflakes or planetary orbits.

So make sure that you pick an appropriate design and don't worry about how simple or obvious it may seem (the pencil, for example). Also be sure that students understand the design you have chosen and that you have given a specific example of it. Be as concrete as possible with your students. For instance, use *World War II* not the concept *War*; use *irrigation* or *cattle raising* or *land terracing* rather than *Agriculture*; or use the *Geneva Convention* or *prisoner's rights* or *apartheid* rather than *Human Rights*.

Students don't have answers to the powerful questions. As awkward as the silences are, wait for answers. Remember that research shows that even a three-second pause can result in an increase in responses from students. Stack papers, walk around the room, or count to ten—do whatever you have to do to give your students time to think and formulate responses. Remember, too, that giving quotas often helps. Ask for a specific number of ideas (three, four, or five) and you are very likely to get them.

Students have too many answers to the powerful questions. If you find that taking every response and writing it on the board takes too much time, there is a way to speed things up without undermining enthusiasm or participation. Simply give fair warning that time is up. Explain that you will take two or three more ideas and then you need to move on. Be sure that you call on each student at some point during the session, but NOT for every question. This will encourage participation and keep things moving at the same time.

Students give inappropriate answers to the questions. Because one purpose of the strategy is to cultivate creative thinking, try not to react at all to silly or unsuitable responses. Do write them on the board, however, as you would any other response. By not reacting negatively, you will be allowing students to feel free to take chances with answers or ideas and you may be pleasantly surprised to find that sometimes the "silly" response generates a good idea. In addition, the inappropriate responses will not get the usual, anticipated attention-getting effect. The exception, of course, is genuine discipline problems which you should deal with as you normally would.

The strategy takes too long. Remember that the time estimates at the beginning of each practice session are realistic. If you find that you are taking much longer and are either pinched for time or are loosing your students' attention, there are several things you can do.

First, try the same approach recommended for situations in which students have too many answers. Set limits on the number of responses you will take and stick to them. Be certain to call on different students throughout the session (rather than after each question) to keep everyone involved.

Second, try having students work on paper or in groups. Doing this will cut down on the amount of time that you spend calling on students and recording their responses. This will also ensure that all stay involved.

If all else fails, you can always trim a lesson down as a last resort. For example, it is better to do just Get Ready, one powerful question, and Think About Thinking than to do nothing at all because of time constraints. Use your best judgment about what to include and what to leave out. You know what your students need to work on most.

The yardsticks are troublesome. The yardsticks are intended to be used as a guide or prompt to extend thinking. If you find that they are becoming a stumbling block, you or your students may be overusing them or using them too literally. Don't worry, for example, about exactly which response fulfills which yardstick. Simply remind students to use the yardsticks if they seem to be unable to move forward with a particular question, or ask them if they have considered the yardsticks, or if the results of their thinking measure up to the yardsticks.